THE WISDOM OF ISRAEL
JOB and PROVERBS

BIBLE GUIDES

The twenty-two volumes

1	THE MAKING OF THE BIBLE	*William Barclay*
2	IN THE BEGINNING	*Bernhard W. Anderson*
3	THE LAW GIVERS	*R. A. Barclay*
4	NATION MAKING	*Lawrence E. Toombs*
5	HISTORIANS OF ISRAEL (1)	*Gordon Robinson*
6	HISTORIANS OF ISRAEL (2)	*Hugh Anderson*
7	PROPHETS OF ISRAEL (1)	*George Knight*
8	PROPHETS OF ISRAEL (2)	*William Neil*
9	PROPHETS OF ISRAEL (3)	*John Mauchline*
10	SINGERS OF ISRAEL	*G. S. Gunn*
11	THE WISDOM OF ISRAEL	*John Paterson*
12	TRACTS FOR THE TIMES	*William McKane*
13	THE GOOD NEWS	*C. L. Mitton*
14	WORLD OF ST. JOHN	*E. Earle Ellis*
15	THE YOUNG CHURCH	*G. E. Ladd*
16	FREEDOM OF THE CHRISTIAN	*F. J. Taylor*
17	PAUL AND HIS CONVERTS	*F. F. Bruce*
18	LETTERS TO THE CHURCHES	*Morton S. Enslin*
19	EPISTLES FROM PRISON	*Donald Guthrie*
20	LETTER TO THE HEBREWS	*William Barclay*
21	GENERAL EPISTLES	*G. R. Beasley-Murray*
22	DREAMS OF THE FUTURE	*T. S. Kepler*

The first four published volumes are:

1. THE MAKING OF THE BIBLE (*William Barclay*), 13. THE GOOD NEWS (*C. L. Mitton*), 11. THE WISDOM OF ISRAEL (*John Paterson*), 7. PROPHETS OF ISRAEL (1) ISAIAH (*George Knight*).

BIBLE GUIDES
General Editors: William Barclay and F. F. Bruce

No. 11

THE WISDOM OF ISRAEL
JOB and PROVERBS

by
JOHN PATERSON
Emeritus Professor of Hebrew and Old Testament Exegesis,
Drew Theological Seminary, Madison N.J. U.S.A.

Published jointly by

LUTTERWORTH PRESS
LONDON

ABINGDON PRESS
NEW YORK AND NASHVILLE

First published 1961

Printed in Great Britain by
Cox & Wyman Ltd., London, Fakenham and Reading

ABBREVIATIONS

R.S.V. (Revised Standard Version of the Bible). The Biblical quotations in this book are from the R.S.V.

A.V. (Authorized Version, or King James Version of the Bible).

GENERAL INTRODUCTION

THE AIM of Bible Guides is to present in 22 volumes a total view of the Bible, and to present the purpose, plan and power of the Scriptures.

Bible Guides are free from the technicalities of Biblical scholarship but are soundly based on all the generally accepted conclusions of modern Bible research.

They are written in clear, simple, straightforward English. Each author has worked to a comprehensive editorial pattern so that the 22 volumes form a concise conspectus of the Bible.

THE AIM

The aim of Bible Guides is to offer a "guide" to the main themes of each book (or group of books) rather than a commentary on the text of the book. Through Bible Guides the Bible itself will speak its message, reveal its power and declare its purpose.

Bible Guides is essentially an undertaking for non-theologically equipped readers who want to know what the Bible is about, how its various parts came to be written and what their meaning is to-day. But the preacher, teacher, educator and expositor of all ranges of the Christian Church will find Bible Guides a series of books to buy and study. They combine the modern knowledge of the Bible together with all the evangelical zeal of sound Biblical expression—and all done in a handy readable compass.

EDITORIAL PLAN

In our suggestions to the writers of the various books we were careful to make the distinction between a "commentary" and a "guide". Our experience is that an adequate commentary on a book of the Bible requires adequate space and on the part of the student some equipment in the scholarly lore and technicalities of Biblical research. A "guide", however, can be both selective and compressed and do what it sets out to do—guide the reader in an understanding of the book. That has been, and is, our aim.

As general editors we have had a good deal of experience among the various schools of Biblical interpretation. We are constantly surprised at the amount of common Biblical understanding which is acceptable to all types of Christian tradition and churchmanship. We hope that our Bible Guides reflect this and that they will be widely used, and welcomed as a contribution to Biblical knowledge and interpretation in the twentieth century.

THE WRITERS

The writers of Bible Guides represent a widely selected area of Biblical scholars, and all of them have co-operated enthusiastically in the editorial plan. They conceive their work to be that of examination, explanation and exposition of the book(s) of the Bible each is writing about. While they have worked loyally to the pattern we suggested they have been completely free in their presentation. Above all, they have remembered the present power and appeal of the Bible, and have tried to present its message and its authority for life to-day. In this sense Bible Guides is, we think, a fresh venture in the popular understanding of the Scriptures, combined as it is with the scholarly skill of our company of writers. We owe our thanks also to our publishers and their editors, Dr. Emory Stevens Bucke of the Abingdon Press of New York and Nashville, and the Rev. Cecil Northcott of the Lutterworth Press of London. Their careful management and attention to publishing detail have given these Bible Guides a world-wide constituency.

WILLIAM BARCLAY

F. F. BRUCE

CONTENTS

INTRODUCTION TO BIBLE GUIDES—THE EDITORS

WISDOM LITERATURE—JOHN PATERSON

THE BOOK OF JOB

1. PURPOSE OF THE BOOK   *Page 13*

A larger thought of God—The life-blood of suffering—A changed view of sin and suffering.

2. PLAN OF THE BOOK   *Page 18*

Folk-tale background—Plan of the poem—A soul's pilgrimage.

3. EXPOSITION OF THE BOOK   *Page 23*

Assembly of the "Sons of God"—Challenge of "the Satan" —Job's friends—rewards and punishment—Job remains unconvinced—Final effort of his friends—Job's outburst of affliction—The upsurge of hope—Job at the turning-point— Love stronger than death—Job's faithful emergence—The Divine speeches—God the voice of a friend.

4. POWER OF THE BOOK   *Page 47*

The eternal background—Reality in religion—The problem of suffering.

THE PROVERBS

1. PURPOSE OF THE BOOK   *Page 53*

Purpose of the Sages—Background of the Sages.

2. PLAN OF THE BOOK   *Page 58*

The eight main sections—Authorship of Proverbs.

3. EXPOSITION OF THE BOOK   *Page 63*

The teachable fool—The hardened fool—The arrogant fool—
Education according to the Sages—Wisdom, president of the
world—The golden mean of moderation—Counsels of the
Sages—The language of the Sages—The place of Proverbs—
Influence on Christian teaching—A manual of ethics.

4. POWER OF THE BOOK   *Page 90*

These timeless counsels—Inherited faith and new dynamic—
The clash of cultures—History is Judgment.

WISDOM LITERATURE

A General View

THE WISDOM LITERATURE of the Old Testament consists of the books of Job, Proverbs and Ecclesiastes, together with some Psalms (1, 37, 49, 73, 112, 119, 127). Outside the Old Testament we have the Apocryphal works of Ecclesiasticus and the Wisdom of Solomon.

Broadly speaking, this Wisdom Literature may be said to represent Hebrew Science and Philosophy, though we must not interpret these terms too literally. The aim of philosophy is the unification of experience, the discovery of certain basic principles which may be manifested in different ways. Thus Natural Philosophy will show that such diverse phenomena as an apple falling from a tree and the movement of the ocean tides are both to be explained by the same principle—the Law of Gravitation. In the same way Moral Philosophy derives right human conduct from a certain number of basic principles such as love, service, and self-denial: these and others will produce the good life according as they are manifested in varying human situations.

Thus the Wisdom Literature represents the effort of the Hebrew mind to understand and explain all that exists. It is the attempt to interpret the facts of life, "to know and to search out and to seek wisdom and the sum of things" (Ecclesiastes 7: 25). But we may not think of these Wise Men as Greek philosophers. The Hebrews did not speculate like Plato or Aristotle. They could not. They were very practical and they "thought with the eye". Theirs was the intuitive type of mind. Their concern was not with the ultimate nature of reality, not with the Being of God—which they assumed—but with forms of His self-manifestation. They were less concerned with the ultimate destiny of man than with the nature of the good life. Hebrew Wisdom always has a distinct religious quality. All the facts of the physical world and all the problems of human life are referred to the divine mind. Human wisdom consists in becoming acquainted with God, in "knowledge of God" or "the fear of the Lord", in yielding to God His due and proper place in human life. Wisdom is occupied with the whole creation: she "rejoices in his inhabited world and delights in the sons of men" (Proverbs 8: 31).

The Two Books

We are here concerned with the books of Proverbs and Job. The former gives a fairly comprehensive practical philosophy of life founded on shrewd observation and based on the firm belief "that God exists, and that he rewards those who seek him". The Book of Job probes deeper and deals with one of the major problems of human life: the Problem of Innocent Suffering. This it does in a concrete practical fashion: its interest is religious rather than intellectual. Only in the latest section of Proverbs and in Ecclesiastes do we find any approach to the abstract method of the Greeks.

Wisdom Literature is not peculiar to the Hebrews. Proverbs and wise sayings emerge in every land where men have eyes to observe. An apparent parallel to the Book of Job has been discovered in Babylon. Egypt, Edom, Tyre, and the children of the East were all famous for wisdom.

The Wisdom writings, with the exception of Job, lack systematic form. They are casual observations rather than an integrated system of doctrine. Most of these writings, though incorporating ancient material, are to be dated in the later period of Israel's history.

JOHN PATERSON

THE BOOK OF JOB

I. PURPOSE OF THE BOOK

THE WISE men or Sages occupied a most significant place in Hebrew life: this we shall see more clearly in our study of the Book of Proverbs. Their function was to interpret the faith of the fathers and to apply it to the changing forms of political and social life. They sought to create a meaningful pattern of life and they did this by the consistent application of religious principles to every aspect of daily life. "The fear of the Lord is the beginning of wisdom", and the word "beginning" here means "prime part" or "foundation". Man's life in all its commonplace details was to be lived in the light of the Eternal and "Man's chief end was to glorify God and enjoy him for ever".

Only so could one find true satisfaction. Inasmuch as the Hebrew was concerned with this life only—the thought of life hereafter did not emerge until late in Hebrew history—the ethics of the Book of Proverbs may seem to us utilitarian and concerned with happiness in this world. They deal mainly with external welfare and material prosperity. The Hebrew judged prosperity to be the fitting reward of piety, as we see clearly in the case of Job. To use the words of Lord Bacon, "Prosperity is the blessing of the Old Testament". That is true and it could not be otherwise. The Hebrew believed in a duly regulated scheme of rewards and punishments because he believed in a righteous God: "Shall not the Judge of all the earth do right?" (Genesis 18: 25.) And for the Hebrew the only sphere in which such righteousness could be revealed was the sphere of time and sense. God must reward the righteous here and now, and here and now He must punish the sinner. In the early period this was probably verified in experience: as in the case of Job, piety was accompanied by prosperity. Any exceptions to the rule were such as proved its truth.

But life does not stand still, not even in the "unchanging East". New conditions emerged to challenge old traditions and accepted customs. It is necessary always to examine our religion and theology lest our formulations thereof and our creeds become outworn and inadequate. Theology and philosophy must continually be confronted with reality and the formula of faith must be set in terms that correspond with reality. Einstein's Theory of Relativity compelled changes in the formulation of many accepted "truths" of Natural Philosophy and Job's final vision enforced a new view of God and His ways with men. And surely no greater service can be rendered a people than the displacement of utilitarian by ideal ethics.

A Larger Thought of God

We shall see that the main purpose of the Book of Job is to enlarge men's thought of God and give them wider horizons, and to assert the rights of the moral personality. *Paradise Lost* was written by John Milton to "assert eternal providence and justify the ways of God to men", and while Job does not range as widely as the Puritan poet his aim is similar. In this book we shall see how man asserts the absolute character of the moral and spiritual against any array of external reasons. Life is more than logic and "the spirit of man is the candle of the Lord" (Proverbs 20: 27). Man's search for final truth will not be denied: God loves an honest thinker. God Himself will endorse the impressive protest against absolutism in theology and He will acknowledge the book's plea for a reasonable service based upon the moral affinity and the mutual understanding of God and man. Job may not go as far as John Stuart Mill in this protest against absolutism but he would have approved Mill's words:

> I will call no being good who is not what I mean when
> I apply that epithet to my fellow-creatures: and if such a

Being can sentence me to hell for not so calling him, to hell I will go.

In this Book of Job a campaign of centuries is dramatically compressed into a single decisive battle. Here the old limited faith gives place to the new, and clearer vision is born, like the fabled phoenix, out of the ashes of the old. There was vast expense of spirit and travail of soul before this poet attained to a place that was luminous with God. This the poet tells us in the book.

The Life-blood of Suffering

We may look for a moment at the context in which this main purpose is worked out. It is a context of history and theology. The Sages, as we see them in Proverbs, did not probe deeply enough and it was left to this poet to deal with a main problem, the problem of innocent suffering. The Sages did not pierce to the centre of things. Life had not dealt too hardly with them and it may be that the insurgent "Why" had been stifled by a comfortable complacency. But Job was no *dilettante*: his faith was not fabricated in the schools of logic but forged in the furnace of affliction. His book is written with his life-blood.

In the changing circumstances of life men failed to observe that it was not always well with the righteous and that the evil-doer did not come invariably to a bad end. Nor could any amount of wishful thinking change the hard brute facts of the matter (Psalm 37). Piety was not always accompanied by prosperity. The fall of the good king Josiah in 609 B.C., to take a conspicuous instance, must have raised serious doubts in many minds and created a real enigma. How can we justify the way of God in such an event? Again, let it be said, our theologies and our philosophies must be adjusted to take in all the known facts so that men may "render a reason for the faith that is in them". Life is no sham fight and no hollow sophistries will avail in the day of the ordeal. The current philosophy found in the Book of Proverbs and elaborated into systematic form in Deuteronomy is here questioned and religion is thrown into the interrogative mood with its cry, "My God, why?" Jeremiah at the end of the seventh century B.C. represents this mood:

Righteous art thou, O Lord, when I complain to thee;
Yet I would plead my case before thee.
Why does the way of the wicked prosper?
Why do all who are treacherous thrive?   (Jeremiah 12 : 1.)

It was right that the current dogma should be questioned, for it had a most grievous corollary. For if prosperity is the sign and seal of piety then suffering and sickness can only be the mark and token of sin. These are the visible evidences of a man's moral rottenness, as material prosperity is the manifest sign of his spiritual soundness. This becomes terribly clear in the Book of Job. Job suffers, therefore Job is a sinner. For *All Sufferers are Sinners*. Job's character is slain by logic. Job might not know of his sin and it might be unknown to his neighbours but it is manifest beyond any doubt by the tell-tale evidence of his suffering. Suffering was not only a physical fact: it was evidence of the divine reaction in wrath against sin. For that reason we find no asceticism or monasticism in the Old Testament. Poverty and pain were to be avoided at all costs, for they were the outward evidence of the divine displeasure.

The tragic element in such a belief, as is clear throughout the book, is that it robbed a man of God and the divine consolations precisely at the point where he most needed these. And it robbed him of the sympathy of his fellow men. Instead he was met with jeers and scorn and regarded as one "smitten of God and afflicted". He became a social pariah: his friends "lifted up their heel" against him and inquired in scorn, "Where is now thy God?" That was the hard flinty theology with which the friends met Job's desperate need, and the purpose of the book is to show what "miserable comforters" they really are. For "miserable" means "needing the mercy of God".

16

A Changed View of Sin and Suffering

Old theologies, like old soldiers, never die. They linger on and surprise us in unexpected places. When the disciples brought the blind man to Jesus their question was "Who did sin, this man or his parents?" (John 9: 2.) They could not think of physical suffering apart from sin. The present writer can attest how such belief prevailed in strongly Calvinistic countries, in the nineteenth century. The San Francisco earthquake, or the eruption of Mount Pelee in the West Indies, presented no problems to some Scots. Were not these people sinners above all men? But facts may not be evaded for ever. The old view must undergo change and development if religion is to retain its hold and if theology is to obtain the approval of men's minds. The faith must be reformulated in terms that include all the facts. Old dogmas must be scrutinized and old creeds confronted with life. Thus it came about that when men looked at Jeremiah and marked the profound passion of his service and the depth of his suffering they could no longer attribute it to sin. As they looked closely at the martyr prophet they reached the conclusion that they could not say "*All Sufferers are Sinners*" but that now, in view of this startling light, they must say, "*Some Sufferers are Saints*". That was advance, and further advance was made when men saw that mysterious figure whom we call the Suffering Servant of the Lord (Isaiah 53). That figure was marred and scarred beyond human recognition: here was suffering on a vast scale. And immediately men thought of sin on the same scale. But a strange new thought entered here. For it is not possible that the eye for ever should cheat the conscience. It was sin, they said, but not his sin. It was their sin that brought this about:

> He was wounded for our transgressions,
>   he was bruised for our iniquities;
> Upon him was the chastisement that made us whole,
>   and with his stripes we are healed.   (Isaiah 53: 5.)

Thus men came to recognize the fact of vicarious suffering, that one might suffer for others. And so they modified the old word and now they said, "*Some Sufferers are Saviours*". Such was the development and a most fruitful development it was. We need not follow it further but we may note that when the apostles sought to interpret the Work of Christ they used the terms applied to the Suffering Servant and showed that the Way of the Cross was God's way to victory.

These developments did not come in a day. Religious institutions are notoriously conservative. Innovations do not enter easily and progress is slow. For Job and his friends there was only that hard barren theology that regarded suffering as the penal judgment upon sin. All these disputants, like the Muslim to-day, were agreed as to the omnipotence of God: they had left no room for His love. Is God's righteousness arbitrary and despotic, or is it morally conditioned? Is man only the plaything of Deity with whom He sports as with Leviathan, or is man a being who can hold communion with his Maker? Is he only God's creature or is he God's friend? These are the questions raised and it is the purpose of the book to answer them.

2. PLAN OF THE BOOK

LIKE MOST of the books of the Old Testament, the Book of Job consists of several sections. The separate sections that have been finally put together give us the book as we now have it:

1. The Prologue   chapters 1: 1–2: 13
2. The Dialogue   ,,   3: 1–31: 40 (except ch. 28)
3. The Speeches of Elihu   ,,   32: 1–37: 24
4. The Divine Speeches   ,,   38: 1–41: 34
5. The Answer of Job   ,,   42: 1–6
6. The Epilogue   ,,   42: 7–17

The Prologue and Epilogue, which make a kind of framework, are written in prose while all that falls between is poetry. The prose sections differ in various ways from the poetical section and these variations concern language, style, and thought. The term *Yahweh* (*the Lord*) occurs 26 times in the framework but only once—and that probably a slip—in the main dialogue. In the framework the narrator is purely objective and writes as an outside observer, while in the poem we have a passionate subjectivity that can be born only out of the poet's own bitter experience. There is anguish here of which the Prologue knows nothing. Nevertheless, there cannot be any doubt that both sections are most closely bound together: the poem without the Prologue would be unintelligible. Without the framework we would not know what it is all about.

Folk-tale Background

Whether one author wrote both the prose and poetical parts may be questioned. There is no reason why a poet should not write prose on occasion and indeed we find in Egypt a work of precisely this same form with a poem enclosed in a prose framework (*Complaint of the Eloquent Peasant*). It would seem more probable, however, that the author of the poem is here using an old folk-tale which told of a righteous man who patiently endured suffering and refused the advice of his wife and friends that he should curse God and die. Scholars judge this folk-tale to have been based on the old doctrine of rewards and punishments, and this judgment seems to be confirmed by the fact that Ezekiel (14: 14, 20) makes reference to Noah, Daniel, and Job as well-known outstanding types of the perfect man. Ezekiel here is referring to the distant past, to something at least earlier than Deuteronomy (621 B.C.) for the old story knows nothing of the law that limited sacrifice to the Temple at Jerusalem. This old story probably originated in Edom and was taken over by the Hebrew writer. It seems to have dealt with the "steadfastness" (R.S.V.) or "patience" (A.V.) of Job (James 5: 11).

It would thus appear that the author of the poem took so much of the old tale as suited his purpose, cut out all in between Prologue and Epilogue, and set in the middle the harrowing story of his own struggle for light. The "patience" of Job may not be too conspicuous in the poem but it was the central subject of the old tale. That is clear from 42:7. We may feel inclined to question the worth of the Epilogue with its stress on material rewards, but probably the author felt it necessary to satisfy popular sentiment in a way they could understand. Everybody wants to be assured that "they lived happily ever afterwards". And after all the Epilogue belongs to the form and artistry of the book, not to its central message.

Concerning the Speeches of Elihu most scholars agree that these form no part of the original work. The dialogue between Job and his friends ends with Job's great "oath of purgation" (ch. 31). There Job makes his final plea for a meeting with God (31: 35—37). The threshold seems set for the divine arrival. Instead, however, enters this somewhat bombastic youth and immediately proceeds to set Job and the friends in their proper place. He thinks he was born to set the world right and he has all the answers. But he adds nothing to what the friends have said, and his entrance halts unduly the whole movement in the region of feeling and emotion and delays the final dénouement. After Job's final appeal we rightly expect the arrival of the divine. And our expectation is justified and right, for in ch. 38 we find no reference to Elihu and what he has spoken. Instead we find a response to the last words of Job:

> Who is this that darkens counsel by
> words without knowledge?
> Gird up your loins like a man,
> I will question you, and you shall declare to me.
>
> (38: 2, 3.)

Nor is there any reference to Elihu in the Epilogue where the friends are condemned. It may be that Elihu felt the poet had failed to offer a solution—and there he was partly right—and

20

he felt that something more should be said. But he fails to add anything save to emphasize Eliphaz's thought that suffering may be disciplinary.

Plan of the Poem

In the poem we find a regular plan. The three friends each speak in turn and Job answers each in turn. This plan proceeds in a threefold cycle but in the third cycle of speeches there has been a serious dislocation of the text. It may have come about accidentally or may be due to carelessness on the part of the copyist. Such things frequently happened: like ourselves they could make mistakes. However it happened we have here something of "a mix-up". Bildad's speech seems unduly brief and Zophar does not appear at all. It has been suggested that this is part of the poet's artistry and that he merely intended to show the friends had run out of arguments. That seems unlikely. Zophar was too much of a dogmatist to be closed out that way and Bildad was not the kind to retire without a final word. So most scholars rearrange these speeches and reapportion the material somewhat as follows:

Eliphaz	ch. 22
Job's Reply	,, 23 : 1–24 : 17, 25
Bildad	,, 25, 26
Job's Reply	,, 27 : 1–12
Zophar	,, 27 : 13–23

No reply is given to Zophar's final blast but in ch. 28 we find a wonderful Poem on Wisdom. This is a magnificent panegyric and, together with Proverbs 8 : 12f., ranks as one of the finest things given us by the Sages. It is, however, completely irrelevant here, for if Job had already attained to this view there would have been no need of the divine Speeches. Job would have perceived what they proclaim. This poem may have been inserted here because Job's answer to Zophar was deemed "unfit to print". We should have been sorry to miss the poem.

But where shall wisdom be found?
    And where is the place of understanding?
Man does not know the way to it,
    and it is not found in the land of the living.
The deep says, "It is not in me",
    and the sea says, "It is not with me".
It cannot be gotten for gold,
    and silver cannot be weighed as its price.
It cannot be valued in the gold of Ophir,
    in precious onyx or sapphire.
Gold and glass cannot equal it,
    nor can it be exchanged for jewels of fine gold.
No mention shall be made of coral or of crystal;
    the price of wisdom is above pearls.
The topaz of Ethiopia cannot compare with it,
    nor can it be valued in pure gold.   (28: 12-19.)

There remain only the divine Speeches. Various objections have been raised here but all scholars are agreed as to the magnificence of their poetry. Some claim to have noted a difference or change in style in the two speeches (38: 1-40: 5, 40: 6-41: 34). The second speech contains two lengthy descriptions of Behemoth and Leviathan which may be pictures of the hippopotamus and the crocodile or mythical creatures. These descriptions are somewhat laboured and in strong contrast to the swift and brilliant pictures of the first divine speech. It must be confessed that Job's submission in 40: 4 affords a most suitable conclusion to the divine response. Moreover, there is always the temptation for a soul sensitive to natural phenomena and sympathetic with the wondrous works of God to expand and add to such descriptions. And if we may speak with reverence one cannot escape the feeling that after Job's penitent submission (40: 4) the second speech looks like "rubbing it in" and a form of nagging which we would scarcely care to associate with the Deity. To many it has seemed that much would be gained by the omission of the second speech although the grounds for doing so are not as compelling as in the case of the Elihu speeches.

Let it be said here that the book of Job is not an easy book to read. Its vocabulary is quite unusual and contains many Aramaic words and also not a few Arabic ones. At times it is hard to make out the exact sense, e.g. 2 : 4, 19 : 25. The Authorized Version is not very helpful but the Revised Standard Version gives more help. The translations of Moffatt or Goodspeed may be consulted with profit.

A Soul's Pilgrimage

What should we call the book? There is a large variety of opinion. It is not an epic, though it has been so called. Nor may we call it a drama in the regular sense of that term. Others have called it a didactic poem. Most writers prefer to say it is in a class by itself for which the usual categories do not apply Perhaps we might best say that here we have the record of a soul's pilgrimage, the history of the poet's own soul, a soul torn by conflicting desires, swayed by alternating hopes and fears, winning its way at last from darkness to light full and clear. Inasmuch as all the movement is within the region of feeling and emotion we may call it a psychological drama.

As to the date, we may be sure it comes from the post-exilic period of the Hebrew people. The fifth century B.C. seems the most probable period though some would date it earlier and others as late as third century B.C. The latter seems hardly possible and the earlier date seems improbable. In view of all the facts we would set it in the fifth century B.C. and nearer the end than the beginning of that century.

3. EXPOSITION OF THE BOOK

THE OPENING verses of the book of Job present us with an idyllic picture in which the manners and customs of the patriarchal age are skilfully delineated. The story belongs to a time before the state had come into being and the life of the family is described in quite imposing fashion. Here we see the background of all that is to follow in the drama. This is the vital situation in which the events narrated took place.

We are introduced to a sheikh, non-Israelite, whose great prosperity, according to the ideas of the period, is matched by his great piety. With meticulous care the "father of the family" acts as high priest for his household of seven sons and three daughters. The home appears to be in Edom, though other situations have been proposed for the land of Uz. "The sons of the East" is a collective name for the Arabic and Aramaic tribes to the N. and N.E. of Palestine. Job's sons appear to be unmarried and lived, like king's sons, each in his own house. Beginning with the eldest a feast was held each day of the week to which all the brothers and sisters were invited. Such is the background of this old folk-tale.

The whole book is concerned with the Problem of Suffering, innocent suffering, and various viewpoints on this matter are offered. It may be best here to deal with each of these viewpoints separately: so shall we reach a greater degree of clarity. This will not be difficult, for each viewpoint can be clearly detached from the others. The Prologue presents one viewpoint peculiar to itself and no reference is made to it in the poem. The speeches of the friends read like separate and distinct disquisitions: Renan spoke of them as "showers of sparks". They develop their arguments with little reference to the case advanced by the other side. A modern poet would certainly have made the speakers submit the contributions of the opponent to a more searching criticism. Similarly Job in his replies contents himself with some sarcastic expressions and straightway proceeds without reference to what the friends have said. He neglects men because he is wholly engaged with God. Thus we shall have little difficulty in making clear the viewpoints of the several participants.

Assembly of the "Sons of God"

The Prologue opens with the picture of the perfect man whose piety is matched by his prosperity: "blameless and upright, one who feared God and turned away from evil", he was blessed with vast outward estate. This was crowned by the domestic joy of a family of seven sons and three daughters. As became a man of such piety he was diligent in the discharge of his religious duty in his home. Every week he was found offering solemn sacrifice to atone for any sins the boys might have committed thoughtlessly. For boys will be boys, and daughters, as the Talmud tells us, are a real source of concern to a man. Job neglects no precaution to ensure that all will be well within his household. Thus did Job continually and walked rightly before God. And God blessed him abundantly.

On a certain day the Lord held audience in His heavenly court and all the ministering spirits who do His pleasure convened in general assembly. For the Hebrew thought of the heavenly King holding court just as do earthly monarchs who regularly call their ministers together to review the general situation. These "sons of God" are not begotten of God in a physical sense: they are beings who belong to the class of *Elohim* (God, divine) just as members of the human race are called "sons of men" (literally "sons of Adam") and members of the prophetic guild were called "sons of the prophets". So also members of the goldsmiths' guild were called "sons of the goldsmith" (Neh. 3 : 8). These celestial beings are God's servants and ministers: at stated times they assemble to do obeisance to their liege Lord and to render an account of their stewardship. As dedicated to the service of God they are called His "holy ones" (5 : 1) though in comparison with God Himself they are considered impure or unwise (4 : 18 ; 15 : 15).

To each of these servants God has allocated a particular function and here we find one singled out as "the Satan", which literally means "the Opposer". We must be careful to note the definite article here: "the Satan" is not the devil as we think of the Evil One. He is a functionary in God's court and all he does is done in strict obedience to God and by divine authority.

The root meaning of the word *Satan* is to oppose or stand over against one. It is the word used in the story of Balaam and his ass where we read in Numbers 22 : 22, 32 that

> The angel of the Lord took his stand in the way
> (literally, stood as a Satan) against him.

It is used all through the Psalms of those who opposed (literally, satanized) the Psalmists. Or more clearly, perhaps, we see the meaning in Zechariah ch. 3 where "the Satan" opposes the claim of Joshua to be high priest in the restored community. "The Satan" is concerned about the shabby garments of this candidate for the high priesthood—the high priest should be properly garbed—and doubts his worthiness to assume this high office. "The Satan" is filled with zeal for God's glory and disturbed lest one unworthy should represent the Most High before men.

Challenge of "the Satan"

It is in this same capacity that "the Satan" appears here in the Prologue. He is the divine superintendent and his district, in which he goes up and down, is the whole wide world. And he moves with searching eyes and inquisitive intent. For he is concerned for God's good name and all too often in his peregrinations he has observed how men make large professions but are really shams and hypocrites. Their practice does not square with their professions. They look good outwardly but within they "are ravening wolves and whited sepulchres". So often has he observed this that he has become completely cynical as to the reality of religion. There is no such thing as pure and disinterested religion. Men do not love God for what He is: they serve Him only for what He gives. "Does Job serve God for nought?" This is a serious indictment of the human race and it must be answered. This is precisely what the old folk-tale set out to do, to refute the sneer and cynicism of "the Satan". We may pause here a moment to say concerning "the Satan" that just as the dyer's hand tends to become subdued to the element in which it works so later we find "the Satan" has deteriorated until finally he becomes an agent opposed to God and the source of evil suggestions (1 Chronicles 21, and cf. with 2 Samuel 24). Later in the New Testament we find him as "the Devil" (*Diabolos*, literally slanderer) : in this way we can understand the "fall of Satan".

The challenge of "the Satan" is taken up by God who looks upon "my servant Job" with admiring pride. The Lord is willing to lay a wager with "the Satan" (quite a few such stories of divine wagers come to us from India) that there is such a thing as real religion and disinterested piety.

Thus the stage is set. Let God strip Job of all his possessions and it will then be seen whether Job's piety will survive the loss of his prosperity. The Lord gives "the Satan" permission to carry out this test. And Job stands the test. All Job's substance is taken from him in a series of dramatic sudden disasters and Job, too, is reft of his seven sons and three daughters. We note this last fact carefully for the disaster happened on the very day on which Job had offered the atoning sacrifice for them, by reason of which they might well be deemed to be in "a state of grace." Ruin was final and complete. "How are the mighty fallen!" Job was brought very low—what did he say?

> Then Job arose, and rent his robe, and shaved
> his head, and fell upon the ground, and worshipped.
> And he said, Naked I came from my mother's womb,
> and naked shall I return : the Lord gave, and the
> Lord has taken away : blessed be the name of the
> Lord. In all this Job did not sin or charge God
> with wrong. (1 : 20–22.)

"The Satan", however, is not so easily discomfited. He has seen too much in his going around to surrender easily his deep-rooted cynicism. And so at the next assembly of "the sons of God" when the Lord points proudly to "my servant Job" and his reaction to the first ordeal "the Satan" is ready with an answer: "Skin for skin—all that a man has he will give for his life." Touch Job in his own person and you will see all his piety melt away. Again the Lord gives permission and "the Satan" goes forth to afflict Job with a deadly disease—it may have been leprosy or elephantiasis. In dire distress Job takes his seat among the ashes while his wife counsels him to curse God and die and be done with it. (The word "curse" is "bless" in the Hebrew: the copyist could not bring himself to write the word "curse" before the word "God".) We can understand the mother, who had just lost her family of ten, speaking thus in frenzy. Her words are to be explained pathologically rather than theologically. And as we listen for Job's reaction to the second test this is what we hear:

> But he said to her, You speak as one of the
> foolish women would speak. Shall we receive good
> at the hand of God, and shall we not receive evil?
> In all this Job did not sin with his lips. (2: 10.)

To Job sitting desolate and forlorn on the ash heap come three friends from afar. They had heard of his grief and they come to sympathize. For seven days and seven nights they sat before him in mute sympathy. "For they saw that his suffering was very great".

We may look at this Prologue and seek its meaning. It may be, as already indicated, that the author of this old tale is indebted to alien sources for this idea of a "divine wager". But be that as it may, the author of this story has here given us something quite different from those other tales. Here he sheds some light or rather offers a viewpoint on the Problem of Suffering. Suffering, he tells us, may have evidential value: it may be a witness to the reality of religion. But the Poet was plainly not satisfied with that viewpoint. After all the discussion here was in heaven and the drama was on earth. It originated in the counsels of heaven and mortal man has no access there. All that was dark both to Job and his friends. "Here we see through a glass, darkly" and must walk by faith. Most of us have seen lives that in the onset of suffering have been "marvellously helped until they were strong" and many of us have visited sickrooms that seemed like the vestibule of heaven, so luminous with God were they. More frequently, however, we have seen lives crushed by suffering until the life has become an agonizing problem as it was to Job. But here we see clearly that suffering may come from God Himself or by His permission and that it may have evidential or testimony value.

Job's Friends—Rewards and Punishment

Now we may look at Job's friends who, like Job himself, believed in the doctrine of rewards and punishments. This belief may be due to the teaching of the great prophets but it was at this time a current doctrine that God rewards the good and punishes the evil. And the Book of Deuteronomy is built mainly on this doctrine. That the friends were faithful to the light they had is clear enough but that they were not open to the reception of further light is equally clear. Theirs is the tragedy of the closed mind: they were static men in a dynamic age. They believed in a God who was but not in a God who was yet to be. Revelation for them was complete and final and the faith once delivered to the saints could suffer no diminution or addition. In their view God had no fresh revelations to break forth from His word. The characters of these friends are fairly distinct. The oldest is Eliphaz, a grey and reverend senior, old enough to be the father of Job. His flinty theology has not robbed him of charity and in all tenderness, as a father with his son, he seeks to deal with Job (4: 2–5). There is here a definite mystical strain and Eliphaz claims to receive direct revelation. In visions of the night the Almighty has spoken with him:

Now a word was brought to me stealthily,
  my ear received the whisper of it.
Amid thoughts from visions of the night,
  when deep sleep falls on men,
Dread came upon me, and trembling,
  which made all my bones shake.
A spirit glided past my face;
  the hair of my flesh stood up.
It stood still,
  but I could not discern its appearance.
A form was before my eyes;
  there was silence, then I heard a voice:
Can mortal man be righteous before God?
  can a man be pure before his Maker?   (4: 12–17.)

The ghostly counsel of Eliphaz, despite its elaborate introduction, fails to make an impression on Job, though often in days gone by Job himself had spoken such words to others. Nor does it in any way ease his situation when Eliphaz suggests the disciplinary and temporary nature of suffering:

Behold, happy is the man whom God reproves;
  therefore despise not the chastening of the Almighty.
For he wounds, but he binds up;
  he smites, but his hands heal. (5: 17, 18.)

Let Job seek unto God in humble penitence and all will be well. Job's latter end shall be greater than his beginning (5: 24–27).

Bildad seems more of a contemporary of Job. He is the scholar of the group. He knows history and all the precedents are at his finger-ends. For him knowledge consists of tradition and his mental furniture consists of proverbs and quotations. Grandfather's religion was good enough for him and it is good enough for Bildad—and it should be good enough for Job. He lacks the tenderness of Eliphaz and he is more concerned to maintain the truth of inherited doctrine. He falls into the fallacy of thinking that because the antediluvians lived longer they should therefore know more than these short-lived ignorant moderns (8:8-10). We should have respect for age and experience. Like a spider's web or a fragile reed is the good fortune of the wicked. God is righteous and the righteous will never be forsaken. Job may yet again enjoy the rewards of his piety. It may be observed here that on the part of the friends there is failure to disengage the righteousness of God from His power and wisdom. More will be heard of this before the debate ends and some theological terms will be re-defined.

The third friend is Zophar and one cannot help wondering how he got into the circle of Job's friends. His mind has no background of mystery and courtesy seems foreign to his nature. He is a plain orthodox dogmatist untroubled by any doubts as to the finality of his faith. He is incensed by Job's protestations of innocence and his cries for more light. Job is just a sophist seeking his own self-justification, a scoffing sinner who is receiving merited punishment from God and kicking against the pricks:

> Know then that God exacts of you less
> than your guilt deserves. (11 : 6.)

Job is but a babbler and "the stupid man must get understanding and the wild ass must be tamed" (11 : 12). It may be that Zophar is aggravated by Job's rejection of the ancient doctrine propounded by the previous speakers. Who does Job think he is? Have not "the divine consolations" been effectual hitherto for such mortal maladies? The patient is just stubborn in refusing his medicine. In any case Zophar does not argue: he simply asserts. Zophar knows well what God would say if He appeared and as He does not appear Zophar will say it for Him.

Job Remains Unconvinced

Thus ends the first cycle of speeches. The current dogma has been stated and re-stated. *All Sufferers are Sinners.* But Job remains unconvinced and unconvicted of sin. Unconscious of

31

any iniquity within himself that could have induced such vast suffering Job holds fast to his integrity. It is the refusal of the friends to face reality and cease repeating shibboleths, which are wholly irrelevant to the case, that vexes Job and us who read the poem. Their minds are fast closed. The new and fuller vision can be reached only through blood, sweat, and tears. A new book of consolation must be written and the friends are not qualified to write it.

So the friends try again. Thus far no formal accusation has been brought, though Job wished they would make specific charges. The primary purpose of the friends was sympathy. But strongly held religious convictions do not generally yield to the promptings of the heart. The "fundamentalist" does not give up easily. Thus we mark a change in the emotional climate as we enter the second cycle of speeches. Eliphaz is more than peeved at Job's seeming irreverence:

> But you are doing away with the fear of God,
>   and hindering meditation before God,
> For your iniquity teaches your mouth,
>   and you choose the tongue of the crafty.
> Your own mouth condemns you, and not I;
>   your own lips testify against you.
> Are you the first man that was born?
>   or were you brought forth before the hills?
> Have you listened in the council of God?
>   and do you limit wisdom to yourself? (15: 4–8.)

Eliphaz here has changed his tune. Consolations and promises should not be wasted upon such a reprobate. Now is the time for threats. The evildoer will finally be overwhelmed by the wrath of God (15: 30f.). Bildad follows in the same line and is both brilliant and truculent. Wounded in his pride he asks if Job takes his friends for beasts that their words are so disparaged and spurned. The brutally unkind reminder of Job's family loss (18: 17) and the reference to his awful disease (18: 13) mark clearly the transition from sympathy to something not unlike hatred. In his profound egoism Bildad would rather see the earth emptied and the rocks removed than admit he is wrong. The last verse (18 : 21) seems to be uttered with an accompanying finger pointed at Job. "As the old cock crows the young one learns" and the tune taken up by Eliphaz and Bildad is carried higher by Zophar. The friends are neither subdued by the exquisite pathos, nor awed by the mighty faith and lofty power of Job's preceding speech. Zophar follows on the soaring vision of Job (ch. 19) with a hot violent harangue which is marked by a fanatical fierceness and unmitigated coarseness that surpasses anything in this moving drama. His frequent reference to snakes may be a clue to his character: he seems to have absorbed some of their venom. His theme is "this is the wicked man's portion from God, the heritage decreed for him by God" (20: 29). When the zealot makes his own opinions and sentiments the measure of God we are likely to get a magnified Zophar on the throne of the universe.

Final Effort of his Friends

Thus we come to the last cycle of speeches. Here there has been dislocation of the text and the only speech unaffected by this confusion is the speech of Eliphaz (ch. 22). This disturbance of the text need not mar the exposition for the friends say the same things. They can make nothing of Job but they have the current dogma behind them and from that they proceed to draw conclusions. Job is a great sufferer, therefore Job is a great sinner. And they proceed to make specific charges against Job. Here, too, they are logical enough for the charges preferred are such as might be made against an opulent oppressor. But in attempting to be logical they only succeed in being fallacious. Eliphaz charges Job with dishonesty, selfishness, cruelty, and avarice. Job thought God does not see these things and that he could get away with them. But sin finds him out and the telltale evidence of his suffering is there to prove it. But history shows that

God abases the proud,
  but he saves the lowly.
He delivers the innocent man;
  You will be delivered through the cleanness of your hands.
                                        (22: 29, 30.)

Bildad follows in a speech apparently mutilated and emphasizes once more the righteousness and power of God and charges Job with sins of omission (chs. 25, 26). All this is logically deduced from the first premiss of the friends. The only trouble here is that the first premiss is false. As a sound scholar Bildad reinforces his argument with parallels from Babylonian mythology (26: 12, 13). Zophar's final blast is made with great gusto and he indicates that Job is the chief of sinners, an object of scorn to God and man.

The final word has been spoken by the friends. Their original sympathetic intent has long since passed from their minds over-whelmed by the demands of their hard stony theology. That theology, however, is subverted and destroyed in the process of the debate: that is surely what the Poet intended. For it has led them to "frame" Job with unsubstantiated charges and to con-demn him on indictments for which there is no evidence, and which are refuted completely by Job's past life and the great oath of purgation (ch. 31). If "hell hath no fury like a woman spurned" the history of ecclesiastical thought might well offer a close parallel in the scorn and hatred of those whose religious tenets have been challenged and spurned. The Poet has made abundantly clear the absurdity of the current doctrine and has shown that "that which is old and ready to perish" must give place to a doctrine more adequate to the interpretation of life.

Job's Outburst of Affliction

We may now turn to Job and mark the movement towards that fuller thought. We will not look for logic here, for Job's wild whirling words are born of affliction and come from one whose ancient faith has been shattered by massive blows. The Poet shows considerable psychological skill in the unfolding of Job's case. For the faith which suffers the first shock of disaster may be unable to abide the continued strain of the dreary after-time. It takes time to realize the magnitude of the disaster and to gauge its full meaning. But grief must sooner or later find expression: only so may the o'ercharged heart find relief.

> After this Job opened his mouth and cursed
> the day of his birth.

As Job realizes the greatness of this catastrophe that has come upon him, the utter hopelessness of his prospect, human nature asserts itself and he breaks out into an exceeding bitter cry. Oh that I had never been born! But having been born, Oh that I might find swift release in welcome death! But let us note here that between the natural cry of despair and a baneful blighting pessimism there is a great gulf fixed. Job does not cross that gulf: Job is no Ecclesiastes. Nor may we forget—and God does not forget—that "the speeches of one that is desperate are as wind" (6: 26). So far the real problem is not yet stated but Eliphaz will raise it for Job. This thing is from God! a punishment from God! That sets Job thinking furiously. Had an enemy done this Job could have understood, but that God should do it to "my servant Job", God with whom he had enjoyed sweet and blessed fellowship—ah, there's the rub! Had God changed his form from that of a friend to that of a fiend? Can such things come to pass? Surely no friend would do this.

Thus Job may speak boldly for he has nothing now to lose. And yet through all this Job feels that his present experience does not reflect God's real attitude to him or reveal God's inmost character. This feeling will grow in Job until it comes to triumphant expression in ch. 19: 25f. Why should God pursue and persecute one so feeble as Job? Once Job knew—and he can never forget it—God's protecting care, but now he knows only torture and trial. Surely it cannot be worth God's while to hound and harry Job as he harried and hunted aforetime the great Leviathan, a foe worthy of the divine steel (9: 13). What is mere man, creature of a day, yea, a maggot and a worm! In a fierce parody of the 8th Psalm (8: 4) Job pictures the Deity as a deadly Grand Inquisitor. Nevertheless, Job cannot forget the blessedness that once he knew and he thinks of God coming again to Job—but Job will be gone and God will be sorry! It will be "too little and too late" (14: 13f.).

The speech of Bildad in ch. 8 introduces a seminal thought, the thought of the divine righteousness, and Job fixes on that thought. We may consider it for a moment. The term "righteous" (*Tsaddiq*) signified originally the victor in a lawsuit, the man who was declared "Right". He might be a real "crook" but in the court the judge awarded him the verdict "Right". And the term rendered "sinner" (*Rasha'*) was applied to the man whose suit was rejected. To him the judge said "Wrong" (*Rasha'*) though that man might be of excellent moral character. Ancient law-courts were subject to bribery and all manner of malpractices: justice was sold to the highest bidder. In later times, however, an ethical sense was imported into these terms and *Tsaddiq* came to signify not the one who received the verdict "Right" but rather the one who should have received it. And *Rasha'* came to signify the man who should have received the verdict "Wrong". Here Job is seizing on the earlier forensic sense and thinking of a legal forum in which God brings charges against him. He does not need Bildad to tell him who will win in such a contest. There can be only one outcome in such a court when puny man contends with the Almighty (9: 15, 16). As in Russian courts to-day, as is commonly reported, he would be forced to condemn himself out of his own mouth:

> Though I am innocent, my own mouth would condemn me;
>> though I am blameless, he would prove me perverse.
> I am blameless; I regard not myself;
>> I loathe my life.
> It is all one: therefore I say,
>> he destroys both the blameless and the wicked. (9: 20, 21.)

The Almighty would intimidate him. Job has no chance.

The Upsurge of Hope

Here in the alternation of hopes and fears comes a gleam of hope. Let God lift His terror for a brief while and Job will speak without fear (9: 33–35). It should be noted that through almost all ch. 9 Job does not use the word "God" but refers only to the terrifying "He". But conscious still of his own integrity and having reached "the dead centre of indifference" he boldly questions the divine righteousness which gives the earth over to injustice, destroying the righteous and mocking the innocent (9: 24). In ch. 10 he reaches the highest point of alienation as he seeks the reason for his suffering: can it be that in a refinement of cruelty the Almighty gave him his former prosperity in order that his subsequent torture might be the more exquisite? Does God really enjoy destroying His own handiwork? Why does He not cease from this malignant persecution and let the sufferer go whence he will no more return? (10: 20f.)

The friends serve as foil to Job and Zophar plants another thought in Job's mind:

> Can you find out the deep things of God?
> Can you find out the limit of the Almighty? (11: 7.)

That thought will lead further, but not yet. Job returns to the thought of a trial and here he makes his plea that God would lift His oppressing hand and let Job speak and God give answer (13: 18–22). This, however, is too much to hope for and Job despairs until another gleam comes to him. Or is it deepening despair?

> For there is hope for a tree,
>   if it be cut down, that it will sprout again,
>   and that its shoots will not cease. . . .
> But man dies, and is laid low;
>   man breathes his last, and where is he? (14: 7, 10.)

Is not man more than a sheep? Is not man more than a tree? We should note the faint upsurge of this hope in Job: it begins small but grows greater, and comes to full expression in 19: 25f. This hope slumbers till Eliphaz speaks again and more sternly than before. In sheer desperation Job is forcing his way towards the light, "an infant crying in the night, an infant crying for the light, and with no language but a cry". Job feels very sure that God cannot really be as the friends describe Him. And there is no flight from God but unto God. His own certainty of moral rectitude and his memories of happier days contribute to this consciousness. To whom can he make appeal (16: 18–21)? Eliphaz' first word that provoked Job's agonizing search now comes to fruition. It is God who has done this, but not the God of the friends who is but a figment of their own imaginations. Job here passes from this low God to the High God of faith who is also the God of fact, from the low God of wrath to the High God of grace:

> O earth, cover not my blood,
>   and let my cry find no resting place.
> Even now, behold, my witness is in heaven,
>   and he that vouches for me is on high.
> My friends scorn me;
>   my eye pours out tears to God,
> That he would maintain the right of a man with God,
>   like that of a man with his neighbour.   (16: 18–21.)

Here we have a real antinomy in the thought of God, a tragic schism set within the divine sphere. That may seem strange to us but it leads Job on his way to the fuller vision. It is akin to the thought of Tennyson:

> Ah yet—I have had some glimmer at times—in my gloomiest woe,
> Of a God behind all—after all—the Great God for aught that I know;

But the God of Love and of Hell together—they cannot be
  thought,
If there be such a God, may the Great God curse him and
  bring him to nought.

"They that seek me shall find me", and verily it is so.

Job at the Turning-Point

Job is now sure that God is his friend, but as that conviction
enters his mind there enters also the haunting fear lest his vindication may not come in his lifetime. Here again hope alternates
with fear. Bildad (ch. 18) provokes Job to deeper despair until
the strain becomes so great that we feel, as the Greek tragedians
felt, that something extraordinary must intervene, or reason will
be lost. Ch. 19 represents Job's darkest hour that comes before
the dawn. We have reached the turning-point. The hand of
God has been heavy upon Job and all his friends have forsaken
him. He is alone in the world, a broken man. In his extremity
his faith performs its greatest miracle, forging for him a creed
which in a sense is the creation of his own spirit, an emanation of
his own character, and at the same time a revelation and dis-
closure from the very heart of God:

        Oh that my words were written!
          Oh that they were inscribed in a book!
        Oh that with an iron pen and lead
          they were graven in the rock for ever!
        For I know that my Redeemer lives,
          and at last he will stand upon the earth;
        And after my skin has been thus destroyed,
          then without my flesh I shall see God,
        Whom I shall see on my side,
          and my eyes shall behold, and not another.
        My heart faints within me! (19: 23–27.)

Here is a marvellous procession of ideas. Job's mind makes a series of lightning-like flights ranging through space and time, earth and heaven, and finally, rending the veil of flesh, stands in imagination, as he will stand one day in fact, face to face with God. The text here is notoriously corrupt but we may not make it say less than the R.S.V. here offers. The words shine like a flight of silver arrows and clearly the thought expressed was exhilarating to Job. "Redeemer" or "Vindicator" renders the Hebrew word "*Gōēl*", and "*Gōēl*" means strictly not so much a Redeemer or Deliverer from sin but a Redeemer of one's honour and Vindicator of one's good name. The *Gōēl* was the nearest kinsman whose sacred duty it was to buy back the person or property—or both—of his kinsman who had fallen into distress or to avenge the blood of a kinsman unjustly slain. Thus in the book of Ruth Boaz acts as *Gōēl* for the Moabite maiden and in Jeremiah ch. 32 Hanamel requests the prophet to discharge the duties of a *Gōēl* and buy his land. A lone woman or a person reduced in circumstances could not very well act for themselves and so the law required that the next-of-kin should discharge a kinsman's duty to the oppressed. Vindica tion and redemption are the ideas involved: the term is used in Isaiah 40–55 of God's redemption of helpless Israel from Babylon. Here Job recognizes that God is not as the friends describe Him but is still as Job knew Him in bygone days:

> Oh, that I were as in the months of old,
>   as in the days when God watched over me,
> When his lamp shone upon my head,
>   and by his light I walked through darkness;
> As I was in my autumn days,
>   when the friendship of God was upon my tent.
>
>   (29: 2–4.)

God will appear again as his friend and plead for him. He will secure his acquittal and vindicate his fair name before the whole

world. In this thought Job leaps the barrier of death: death will
not rob him of his final satisfaction.

Love Stronger than Death

This may not be construed as a doctrine of immortality,
though some scholars read it so. But it surely expresses the assur-
ance that the love of God is stronger than death and that death
will not sever his friendship with God. And that surely is one
factor in any doctrine of immortality. It would seem that in
this Job's darkest hour the veil was for a moment rent and that
Job saw to the other side of things. And surely for all of us
heaven will just be seeing the other side of things, the things we
could not see here nor understand. And the things we see in
such rare ecstatic vision, as Paul tells us (2 Corinthians 12: 4),
we cannot utter. But the vision satisfies beyond the power of
frail mortal speech to express. "My heart faints within me!"
But though heart and flesh faint and fail, as the Psalmist says, the
Lord is my portion and my strength for ever. *There are some
things too good not to be true.* This is one of such things. It makes
all the difference to Job, as we can perceive from the change of
mood that becomes apparent at this point. The emotional
strain is relaxed, for Job's personal problem is solved though the
larger problem of world order remains. The friends remain and
through the last cycle they will maintain the method of the
mosquito. But they cannot rob Job of his vision, and though he
must linger yet awhile amid the smoke and dust of the arena he
will not forget his vision.

The problem of the general world government remains.

> Why do the wicked live,
>   reach old age, and grow mighty in power?
> Their children are established in their presence,
>   and their offspring before their eyes.
> Their houses are safe from fear,
>   and no rod of God is upon them. (21: 7–9.)

The facts of life are there for all to see. It is not true that the righteous flourish like the green bay tree and that the wicked are swept away as chaff before the wind (21: 17, 18). The problem vexes Job and in ch. 23 he again expresses a passionate plea to come before God (23: 3–9). He would fain reason the matter with God—and surely God is essentially reasonable. The friends have ceased to concern him in any way: his business is with larger issues than the opinions of men. To all their suspicions and misrepresentations he opposes not only the reticence of moral strength but the fortitude of an instinctive faith. The friends, however, still serve a purpose in that by questioning his integrity they force Job to turn Godwards. And this is not in vain; for the undimmed light of his moral consciousness illumines for him the way that leads to God. He shall yet come forth from the ordeal as gold tried in the fire.

Job's Faithful Emergence

We can pass by the last broken cycle of speeches where we see Job finally "emerging into the clear". Ch. 29 will recall the joys of yesteryear and give a foretaste of joys to come, while ch. 30 will show how "sorrow's crown of sorrow is remembering happier things". But if Memory may be Hell it may also be Heaven. In ch. 31 comes the great oath of purgation where Job lays his life as an open book before God and men. Nowhere in the Old Testament do we find so high a statement of ethical principle and nowhere—not even in the Decalogue—do we so closely approximate the New Testament ethic. This might seem to savour of Pharisaism but for the intense moral and spiritual passion with which the declaration is charged. Life is laid here before God and the record is shown in the light of the eternal.

If I have rejected the cause of my manservant or my maid-
    servant, when they brought a complaint against me;
What then shall I do when God rises up?

> when he makes inquiry, what shall I answer him?
> Did not he who made me in the womb make him?
> and did not one fashion us in the womb?   (31: 13–15.)

Here is respect for man as man and no room is left for discrimination, segregation, or social distinction. Morality is not an external adornment which one assumes but the spontaneous outflow of a heart totally committed to God and His demands. "As a man thinketh in his heart, so is he." Here is a man whose life is rooted and grounded in God, and the fruits of that life are plain for all to see. With absolute sense of moral rectitude he stands before God and awaits the entrance of the divine:

> Oh, that I had one to hear me!
> (Here is my signature! let the Almighty answer me!)
>   Oh, that I had the indictment written by my adversary!
> Surely I would carry it on my shoulder;
>   I would bind it on me as a crown;
> I would give him an account of all my steps;
>   like a prince I would approach him.   (31: 35–37.)

Bloody but unbowed Job stands at the threshold of the divine arrival.

The Divine Speeches

We need not delay with the speeches of Elihu, which we have seen reason to regard as an intrusion in the work. Nothing new is added there though he dwells more fully on the disciplinary aspect of suffering (ch. 33), a thought first suggested by Eliphaz (5: 17). Thus without more ado we pass to the divine Speeches.

As already indicated these speeches seem to have been expanded by a later hand: from an artistic viewpoint the first speech seems sufficient and conclusive. Ch. 31 ends with Job's plea for an answer from God and confident as a prince he awaits a reply. Now the Almighty appears in all the power and glory

of the universe, more exalted and majestic than Job had ever
dreamed, and speaks out of the thundercloud:

> Who is this that darkens counsel by
>   words without knowledge?
> Gird up your loins like a man,
>   I will question you, and you shall declare to me.
>
> (38: 2, 3.)

It is a strange speech and the opening must have daunted Job
a little. It certainly puts him at another point of view than that of a
prince. But this was necessary. Job had been speaking without
full knowledge, from a narrow and limited viewpoint, the viewpoint of the old dogma. Now a larger framework is being
offered and the problem is shown in its proper context. The
divine speaker says nothing of retribution and he ignores all the
friends' accusations and Job's defence. The speaker scarcely
seems to touch the problem that has so provoked their fury and
debate. Nevertheless, Job is awakened as from a nightmare
dream to find himself in a larger world, a gracious world, full of
reason and full of consolation. Here he learns that help and
comfort will come to him by the exercise of his own reason and
thought. He learns that the finite cannot comprehend the In-
finite and that God's greatness outreaches all our feeble thinking
and leaves our poor imaginations far behind. He learns, too,
that we cannot lay a line upon all the tender compassions of our
God. He it is who

> provides for the raven its prey,
>   when its young ones cry to God,
>   and wander about for lack of food.
>
> (38: 41.)

and He it is who sends

> rain on a land where no man is,
>   on the desert in which there is no man.   (38: 26.)

This reminds us of the Gospel where we read that nothing in all God's world—not even a sparrow—is untended by His care, unmarked by His grace. That was what Job wanted to know: does God care?

> From the first, Power was, I knew;
> Life has made clear to me,
> That strive but for a closer view,
> Love were as plain to see.   (Browning.)

From the narrow chaotic world of life's uncertainties Job is brought into a large place, a cosmos that is radiant with God. He is lifted "into the heavenlies" where all problems cease to vex. His former discontent is swallowed up of the beatific vision: his heart is at peace. God gives no explanation but to the anguished spirit He gives such a vision of divine power and grace that questions cease in the peace of humble submission. Was not this the experience of Saint Paul in his suffering?

> Three times I besought the Lord about this,
> that it should leave me; but he said to me,
> My grace is sufficient for you, for my power
> is made perfect in weakness.   (2 Corinthians 12: 8.)

God does not answer the hot dusty interrogations of the mind but He does satisfy the profound yearnings of the spirit.

God the Voice of a Friend

From his dark doubts Job is lifted into the upper world to hear the music of the spheres and to find in the great harmony of the universe a rebuke to his groundless perturbation and a fresh sense of the glory and goodness of God. This is the voice of a Friend, and now he knows that if God has cast him down it was only that He might raise him up in the strength of implicit trust. The

45

great God of righteousness, mercy, and truth reveals Himself as He really is. Job seeks nothing more.

> Behold, I am of small account;
>   What shall I answer thee?
> I lay my hand on my mouth.
> I had heard of thee by the hearing of the ear,
>   but now my eye sees thee;
> Therefore I despise myself,
>   and repent in dust and ashes.   (40: 4, 42: 5.)

Sorrow is forgotten in the revelation of God's loving kindness and Job's humble submission is of that high order that passes into boundless joy.

Job's pain and suffering are not removed or subtracted. But something new has been added in presence of which his pain will not be so much as spoken of or remembered. "My grace is sufficient for thee." All pain is turned to peace and his heart rests in the beatific vision. The weeping that endured for a night has been transformed into the joy of morning.

And God is proud of "my servant Job" who has "spoken of me what is right". And Job's sacrifice and prayer will avail for the friends who "have not spoken of me what is right". The Epilogue may seem to us a piece of anticlimax but the author felt it necessary for the artistry of his work. Job's vindication must be made clear to lesser souls who could not climb such spiritual heights, and who could be convinced only by material things. The rings of gold and pieces of money and the daughters with the high-sounding names must have seemed as vanity to Job who had pierced to the centre of things and found God. For when once a man stands face to face with God and learns what God really is all other arguments and illustrations are unnecessary. It is the direct and immediate experience of God that satisfies, and not the evidence of men concerning Him. Having Him we have all and are "more than conquerors".

4. POWER OF THE BOOK

THERE MAY be diverse opinions as to the structure of this book but there is unanimity as to its quality as literature. It stands pre-eminent by the judgment of all. Luther judged it "magnificent and sublime" while Herder, a master in literary appreciation, called it "regal and sublime". Bishop Lowth, a master in the matter of Hebrew poetry, held it to be "unparalleled in the sacred volume": to Renan it was the Hebrew book *par excellence*: "here the force, the beauty, the depth of the Hebrew genius are seen at their best". A. B. Davidson called it "the most splendid creation of Hebrew poetry", while A. B. Bruce maintained "there is nothing like it, either in the Bible or out of it, nothing so thorough, so searching, and so bold". Let these tributes suffice. The Book of Job finds us in the deepest parts of our being and we thrill to it. That is the test of great literature.

There is not so much great literature, John Morley once said, "Literature consists of all the books—and they are not many—where moral truth and human passion are touched with a certain largeness, sanity, and attraction of form."

We may ask how many books answer these demands. Precious few. All would agree on Homer's *Iliad,* and none would dissent from Dante's *Divine Comedy* or Shakespeare's plays. Perhaps Plato's *Dialogues* or the Greek tragedians or Goethe's *Faust* might seem worthy of a place, though many would raise a question there. But none will question the right of the "big three" mentioned. There is something in each of these, from the ancient, mediaeval, and modern periods, that marks them out as distinct. They stand beside the Bible as great literature. In them is quality, the rhythm of great music, the grace of a polished shaft, and winged words that have tints as well as tones, that ring like iron and shine like cloth of gold. Truth unadorned does not live in the memory of man but truth shaped and glowing with beauty lays a spell on all the generations. Truth wedded to beauty creates immortal literature.

For these immortals see life steadily and they see it whole. Here are wide horizons, penetrating insights, and amplitude of diction. Nothing low or mean is here. Theirs is the vision splendid and the background is eternal. Dante will range the cavernous depths of hell and he will read man's life in the face of God. The crowded stage of Shakespeare will disclose a world of manifold emotions comparable to that of Holy Writ. None will surpass this bard in his austere view of the grandeur of the Moral Law. Homer's battles on the windy plains of Troy are appointed and determined by the high gods of lofty Olympus. The background is the eternal. And nowhere, save in the Bible, is that background so patent and clear. The Hebrew word "it-came-to-pass" sums up this whole matter. Men come and men pass. Only God abides "from everlasting to everlasting". This eternal background gives meaning to history and significance to human life.

The Eternal Background

Such is the background of Job and his book. And it is the background of his suffering. That suffering is appointed in the eternal counsels of God. It originates in heaven. This is the abiding mystery of life and constitutes the real problem for Theism. Why does a God of love permit such suffering? Much can be explained as the friends did, but not all. For much suffering is the inexorable outcome of sin. But we may not say *All Sufferers are Sinners*. There is much suffering that is without obvious reason. Such is Job's suffering, the reason for which was known only to the heavenly council. Job's suffering was sent upon him to discredit the base cynicism of the Satan and to prove the reality of disinterested religion. In this sense Job is God's champion. And God is willing "to bet his life" on Job's piety. We may be certain that the heart of God was sorely grieved in this ordeal of Job. In all Job's afflictions He was afflicted. It is worth noting that while we make much of our faith in God—and rightly so—there is another side to this matter. God has faith in us. He believes that we will not let Him down or prove recreant. And it is the blood of the martyrs (martyr means faithful witness) and not the ink of our theologies that is the seed of the Church. God is proud of Job in the Prologue and prouder still in the Epilogue.

Reality in Religion

For God loves an honest thinker. God loves reality in religion. Our service is to be with our whole heart and soul *and mind* and strength. Job serves with his mind. He believes that God is rational and reasonable. "Come now, let us reason together" (Isaiah 1 : 18). It is no fool or arbitrary despot that sits on the throne of the universe, although Job comes perilously near to suggesting that. But God, precisely because He is reasonable, will not and does not hold Job's wild whirling words against him. God knows, as the friends know not, that these words are the words of a desperate man, a man desperate to attain the truth. No second-hand opinions will avail here : nothing but ultimate truth will satisfy Job's agonizing search. That truth is reached only through vast expense of spirit and sweat of heart and head. And that God approves such honest thinking is clear from the Epilogue. It was not the friends who said the right things about God : it was the man who said the terrible shocking things in the desperate honesty of his soul who won the divine approval.

It is the more necessary to say this in that Job's friends are not yet dead. They have simply changed their form and in our day they appear in the guise of the "honest doubter". There is a tendency to-day to prefer the honest doubter to the real believer. Two things should be said here. Firstly, there is much to be said for a reverent agnosticism in presence of this problem, but the fact that we cannot know everything should not preclude us from learning and getting to know all we can. The position of

49

"honest doubt" implies indecision, uncertainty, and it must always involve agony if the doubt is honest. Our prayer here must be, "Lord, I believe, help thou mine unbelief". God will hold certain forms of doubt to be culpable and both God and Job would repudiate this tendency to regard the "honest doubter" as a kind of superior person. Doubt is not a thing to be bragged about, and this flippant way of speaking is much to be deplored. And, secondly, all too often it will be found that this "honest doubt" is no more than a smokescreen thrown up to hide an evil heart and cover a reluctant will. Doubt when it is honest is an agonizing thing, as we see in Job and may have felt in our own lives, and it will give the doubter no rest until he finds rest in God. This is the ministry of God's own Holy Spirit. We must see to it that our righteousness exceeds that of self-deluding optimists and those who put on blinders.

The Problem of Suffering

We may pass now from the sufferer to his problem. The Problem of Suffering is perennial and the last word has not yet been spoken. But we have inherited the thoughts of honest thinkers and we build on them. About the same time as our book was written another voice was raising the question. That voice is heard in Isaiah 40–55 and it is the voice of the Suffering Servant of the Lord. In Isaiah ch. 53 we come by another view of suffering: suffering has vicarious power. It may seem strange that our Poet did not refer to this view of the matter:

> He was wounded for our transgressions,
>   he was bruised for our iniquities;
> upon him was the chastisement that made us whole,
>   and with his stripes we are healed.   (Isaiah 53 : 5.)

It may be he did not know of this voice, though that seems unlikely. Or it may be that he felt it irrelevant in the individual case of Job. In this song Isaiah regards suffering as an offering for sin while the author of Job viewed it as the vindication of the divine honour and disinterested religion. Perhaps the two views are not so far apart. Job's piety and prayers availed for his friends while the Servant "by his righteousness justifies many".

The Old Testament asks questions and the New Testament gives the answers. Religion in the interrogative mood is matched with religion in the affirmative; the positive splendours of the New stand over against the interrogations of the Old Testament. Job's pathetic cry for a "daysman" or "umpire" (9: 33) has been answered. "The Word became flesh and dwelt among us . . . and from his fulness have we all received, grace upon grace" (John 1: 14, 16). The Incarnation and the Death of Christ have shown that suffering is not merely a human experience: it is in the heart of God Himself. Pain and suffering have meaning and that meaning is made clear in the Cross. To know Jesus is to know God: when we see Jesus we can say with Job, "Now mine eye seeth thee".

The sufferings of Christ have vicarious power. "He was bruised for our iniquities." By His sorrow we have rest and life by His death. The Royal Way of the Holy Cross, to use the words of Thomas à Kempis, is the way of triumph both for God and man. The Cross is set at the centre of our Christian life of service and sacrifice. God hides a gospel in our pain and builds our most abiding joys upon our suffering. The first church this writer served in Scotland bore the motto, cut in the stone, "No Cross, no crown". That is the law of our life. We share in the fellowship of His sufferings and fill up that which is behindhand in the suffering of our Lord (Colossians 1: 24). Not that Christ failed to offer a complete and perfect oblation, once and for all, but that through His complete identification with us He makes our sacrifice His own. For our sake God "made him to be sin who knew no sin, so that in him we might become the righteousness of God" (2 Corinthians 5: 21). He was "numbered with the transgressors" that the transgressors might be numbered with the saints. He dwells in us and our life "is rooted and grounded in God". And if we share the fellowship

51

of His sufferings we shall also share the fellowship of His glory. Thus our sufferings, being taken up into His, have vicarious power. And for the vague hope that flickered before the eyes of Job we have a hope that is sure and certain. "This slight momentary affliction is preparing for us an eternal weight of glory" (2 Corinthians 4 : 17). In the larger and wider context we see clearly and are satisfied with what we see. With Paul we can say :

> In all these things we are more than conquerors
> through him who loved us.
> For I am sure that neither death, nor life, nor
> angels, nor principalities, nor things present,
> nor things to come, nor powers, nor height, nor depth, nor
> anything else in all creation, will be able to separ-
> ate us from the love of God in Christ Jesus
> our Lord.   (Romans 8 : 37, 38.)

THE PROVERBS

"ALL SCRIPTURE is inspired by God and profitable for teaching, for reproof, for correction, and for training in right-eousness, that the man of God may be complete, equipped for every good work." So wrote Paul to Timothy (2 Timothy 3 : 16) and such a statement may well receive our assent. For the Bible is not a scientific textbook. It does not tell us how the heavens go but it tells us how we may go to heaven. It was written "to make us wise unto salvation "and its main purpose is the for-mation of character.

The real meaning of the Hebrew word "Wisdom" (*Chokmah*) is "strong" or "firm" and the verb means to make strong and sound. Nowhere is this purpose clearer than in the book of Pro-verbs. In no other book do we find so frequently those words mentioned by Paul, "correction", "reproof", "training". This is pre-eminently a book of religious education and its purpose is to shape and mould sound character:

> That men may know wisdom and instruction,
>> understand words of insight,
>> receive instruction in wise dealing,
>> righteousness, justice, and equity;
> that prudence may be given to the simple,
>> knowledge and discretion to the youth.　(1 : 2–4.)

This book has played a large part in the formation of national character: its precepts have been imbibed by Americans as well as Scots, while John Ruskin, the English writer, tells us he pre-ferred it above all other books of the Bible. In our day when most discerning folk have a profound concern for the decay of character and the necessity of sound education the study of this book may be timely and rewarding. With all our getting we must not fail to get wisdom. The Sages in ancient times saw this as a paramount need and set themselves to meet this need.

Purpose of the Sages

This purpose is clear from the outset. The wise man and the fool appear on almost every page of this book and we learn right away that the aim of these Sages was to subtract from the number of fools and add to the number of the wise. They sought to educate for life. That is the aim of every wise educator and of every good minister. Their aim is expressed in the words engraven in Hebrew letters on Andrew Bonar's church in Glasgow: "He is wise that winneth souls" (11: 30). For this reason they sought conversions with unremitting zeal. Their methods, at times, might seem somewhat unorthodox but perhaps we make too much of orthodoxy. Perhaps to-day we need less orthodoxy and more flexibility in our approach to this question: we might well take a leaf from the book of Paul (I Corinthians 9: 22) or the adventurous John Wesley. Both prophets and priests might look askance at these practitioners who were not "in holy orders". These Sages had the character of freelances but none could doubt their unswerving loyalty to the heritage that had made Israel the people of God. And the Sages believed that heritage was for all men. Their parish was the world and their message was for Everyman. Many of these Sages had travelled abroad and seen other men and other manners: their minds were liberated from narrow national prejudices. They represent the finest education of their period in combination with the pious spirit of their religion. They shared fully in the international exchange of ideas and their viewpoint was ecumenical. They counted nothing human alien to them. In a day when foreign fashions were threatening to overwhelm the moral and spiritual life of their people they stood forth to "reprove, correct, and equip men for salvation". For they knew "those things by which men live and wholly therein is the life of the spirit" (Isaiah 38 : 16).

Background of the Sages

We may pause here to look at those Wise Men or Sages who espoused and carried through this lofty purpose. Who were the Sages? They come into prominence somewhat late in Hebrew history but they have their roots in the early period. It is generally agreed that they are closely related to the earlier government "scribe" (A.V.) or "secretary" (R.S.V.) concerning whom we read in 2 Samuel 8 : 17; 20 : 25; 1 Kings 4 : 3; 2 Kings 19 : 2; 22 : 3–7; Jeremiah 36 : 20, 21. These were government secretaries and they must have been men of capacity and experience. From Egypt and Babylon we learn a good deal about such men and in this matter Israel owed more to Egypt than to Babylon. Babylon was the centre of big business and was given more to action than to reflection. Egypt was more relaxed and could "sit still" by the Nile and take time to think of things. Thus we find a considerable volume of Wisdom Literature from Egypt, dating back millennia before Christ. This Wisdom, it is true, is mainly prudential and is directed to a special group, the career men in the government service. We have here the work of Ptah-hotep (about 2450 B.C.) and we see how he is anxious to train suitable successors: his counsels are mainly directed to instructing younger men how to win friends and influence people.

We may find much similar to this in the book of Proverbs and we shall note that quite a large piece of Egyptian wisdom has been incorporated in our book of Proverbs (p. 61). Such men were found in Israel and we may recall Ahithophel whose counsel was reputed to be as "the oracle of God" (2 Samuel 16 : 23). But these men were mainly politicians with their ear to the ground and their eye on the main chance. And too often it might be said, as it was said, that "this time the counsel which Ahithophel has given is not good" (2 Samuel 17 : 7). And if Ahithophel had imbibed some of the counsels of this book of Proverbs he might not have come to the bad end he finally met (2 Samuel 17: 23). There were various kinds of counsel: politicians were apt to give counsels of expediency and neglect sound moral principle. Isaiah may have had these in mind when he wrote:

> Woe to those who are wise in their own eyes,
>> and shrewd in their own sight!   (Isaiah 5: 21.)

For surely as "the fear of the Lord is the beginning of wisdom",

> The wisdom of their wise men shall perish,
>> and the discernment of their discerning men shall be hid.
>>> (Isaiah 29: 14.)

Like prophecy in Israel which moved from its crude beginnings upward to the splendour of eight- and seventh-century prophecy, so Wisdom developed from rather shady forms and practices to the higher form represented by Proverbs. The development is not quite clear but its main lines can be discerned. It may be that during the monarchy men from official circles formed themselves into a distinct body and became counsellors or Sages (*Chakamim*). The process may have been more gradual and more casual. We might think of retired civil servants who loved their nation, who had travelled and gained experience, and were now willing in their leisure to impart their experience and judgment to others. Such persons were well qualified to speak with authority and Ecclesiasticus is probably thinking of such when he writes:

> He serveth among great men,
>> and appeareth before a ruler;
> He travelleth in the land of foreign nations,
>> and hath experience of both good and evil among men.
>>> (Ecclesiasticus 39: 4.)

Though the Sages say little or nothing about Jewish ritual we may not conclude, as many do, that here we are dealing with wisdom like that of Ptah-hotep or the Hebrew state secretaries. Right in the forefront and all through the book runs the refrain, "The fear of the Lord is the beginning of wisdom", and "beginning" (rēshīth) means "prime element" or "foundation". The *religious emphasis* is pervasive and predominant. Hebrew does not have a word for "religion" but it has useful synonyms like "the fear of the Lord" or "the knowledge of God". These terms include all we mean by the term "religion". The purpose of the Sages was to demonstrate that religion was concerned with a man's whole life and that it involved total commitment. Like Paul they urged men that

> whether you eat or drink, or whatever you do,
> do all to the glory of God.   (1 Corinthians 10: 31.)

All life was to be integrated in His service and all the unredeemed aspects of life were to be brought within the religious sphere.

"The Sages" supplemented the ministry of the Priests: theirs was a roving ministry untied to any institution. At street corners, in the public squares, as visitors in synagogues or guests in a home they were free to speak their piece. Both Priest and Sage regarded religion as a rational relationship to God and both believed in the moral government of the world. In the period after Ezra the Sage changed character to a degree and occupied himself, as a scribe, with the text of the Law (*Torah*), which he interpreted in most literal and pedantic fashion. The wider horizons of the earlier period were lost and the Law of Moses came to be regarded as the sole source of Wisdom. The basis of the teaching was narrowed but the purpose remained the same.

The Sages were in fundamental agreement with the Prophets. It was not given to the Sages to breathe the ampler ether and diviner air where the prophets moved and to share the secrets of the Almighty. The prophets were somewhat remote figures with an air of elevation about them, but the Sages were creatures of flesh and blood, always accessible and ready to meet their fellow men on the level. They could sit where common folk sat and for such they "broke down small" the lofty message of the prophets that truth might enter in at lowly doors. They were religious middlemen and mediated the prophetic word to the man in the street.

"In many and various ways God spoke of old to our fathers" (Hebrews 1 : 1). One way was the way of the Sages. That their ministry was not ineffectual or unblessed is clear from Israel's later history and the records of more recent times. Their purpose to "reprove, correct, instruct" can never be fruitless, and Daniel, the ideal Jew, surely had such in mind when he wrote:

Those who are wise shall shine like the brightness of the
   firmament;
   and those who turn many to righteousness, like
   the stars for ever and ever.   (Daniel 12 : 3.)

2. PLAN OF THE BOOK

THE FULL title of the book is "the Proverbs of Solomon, son of David, king of Israel". The Hebrew word for proverb is *mashal,* and that word has a somewhat extended meaning. It is applied to the *oracles* of Balaam (Numbers 24 : 15) and in the R.S.V. it is translated by the English word *discourse.* It is used in Isaiah 14 : 4, Habakkuk 2 : 6 and is there translated by the R.S.V. as *taunt* while in Ezekiel 17 : 2, 20 : 49, 24 : 3 it is translated (R.S.V.) as *allegory.* The original meaning of the word seems to be that of comparison, laying one thing alongside another, as in Genesis 10 : 9, "Like Nimrod a mighty hunter before the Lord", or

Like vinegar to the teeth, and smoke to the eyes,
So is the sluggard to those who send him.
                          (Proverbs 10 : 26.)

It is not difficult to see how this could be widened to the sense of parable or allegory.

The Eight Main Sections

The book is made up of various collections and just as in the Psalter so here also we find duplicates or doublets, the same proverb repeated in different collections. The whole book may be divided as follows:

I. 1:1——9:18, The Proverbs of Solomon, son of David, king of Israel.

II. 10:1——22:16, The Proverbs of Solomon.

III. 22:17——24:22, The Words of the Wise.

IV. 24:23–34, These also are the Sayings of the Wise.

V. 25:1——29:27, These also are proverbs of Solomon which the men of Hezekiah, king of Judah, copied.

VI. 30:1–33, The Words of Agur, son of Jaken, of Massa.

VII. 31:1–9, The Words of Lemuel, king of Massa, which his mother taught him.

VIII. 31:10–31, Praise of the Good Wife.

Section I, strange as it may seem, is probably the latest part of the book. The first six verses seem to be an introduction to the whole book as we now have it, and this book was not assembled until late in the post-exilic period—the exile ended about 540 B.C. The material in this collection consists mainly of little essays interspersed with an occasional brief wisdom saying or *gnome*. In chapter 8 occurs a remarkable personalization of Wisdom and this may be one of the main sources of John's thought of the Word made flesh (John 1:14). Such advanced theological thought did not emerge in the earlier period of Israel's history: both the literary form and the developed theology of this section seem to indicate a date in the third century B.C. The whole section is very similar to the book of Ecclesiasticus written in Hebrew about 192 B.C. and translated into Greek in 132 B.C. This does not mean that older material may not be included in this section.

Section II is generally regarded as the oldest part of the book and here much preliterary material may be preserved, sayings not as yet written down but preserved by oral tradition. Here we have a total of 375 proverbs, generally quite separated and un-related. Sometimes they may be connected by a common view-point or formal likeness, e.g. 10: 2, 3; 10: 4, 5; 10: 6, 7; 16: 10–15 (all concerning kings), and 11: 9–12 where four couplets all begin with the Hebrew letter "B". It may be pointed out in passing that the letters of the Hebrew alphabet also represented numbers and that the letters forming the name "Solomon" add up to 375. In this collection we have mainly self-contained couplets set in various forms of parallelism. In chapters 10–15 the form of parallelism is usually antithetic, the form in which the thought is set forth by contrast or antithesis:

> A wise son makes a glad father,
>> but a foolish son is a sorrow to his mother. (10: 1.)

In chapters 16–22: 16 we find generally synonymous parallelism where the thought is set forth by repetition:

> A just balance and scales are the Lord's,
>> all the weights in the bag are his work. (16: 11.)

Again the thought may be set forth in simple comparison:

> Better is a little with righteousness
>> than great revenues with injustice. (16: 8.)

Or by ascending parallelism where one thought is added to another:

A hoary head is a crown of glory;
it is gained in a righteous life.   (16: 31.)

The last example might suggest the question whether some of
these couplets were not originally single-line sayings and that
the second line was added to give literary form. The proverbs
in this oldest collection reflect conditions prevailing in a time of
comparative peace and material prosperity when life was simple
and the main work was cultivation of the soil. The Sayings of
the Wise found ready acceptance in a community without any
high degree of sophistication. Family life was pure, the mother
was honored (12: 4; 18: 22; 19: 14), parental authority was
upheld, and the king was respected as God's anointed (21: 1).
The collection reflects the happier conditions of the early monarchy.

   Section III (22: 17–24: 22) may be subdivided into 22: 17–23:
14 and 23: 15–24: 22. The former collection is clearly indebted
to the Wisdom of Amenemope (800 B.C.) and seems to have
been "lifted" straight from that Egyptian sage. The "excellent
things" of 22: 20 (A.V.) had long been a stumbling-block to
translators but is no longer so. "The thirty sayings" (R.S.V.)
is correct, for this is what Amenemope wrote, "Consider these
30 chapters". The writer has considered them well and in these
sayings of which he gives exactly 30, he reproduces Amenemope
in 23 of them. (The text of Amenemope and the parallel verses
of this section are set forth in parallel columns in the West-
minster commentary of W. O. E. Oesterley.) *Section IV* may
be regarded as an appendix to the third collection: it consists of
five brief sayings warning against partiality and laziness. Both
these sections may be considered pre-exilic but may not be dated
before 700 B.C. *Section V* (25: 1–29: 27) is to be assigned to the
period of Hezekiah; it contains 138 verses of which 128 are in
couplet form. Perhaps here we have a merging of two smaller
separate collections. In chapters 28, 29 we have couplets only
and the religious element is more strongly stressed.

   Sections VI, VII and VIII. That they are separate collections is clear from the fact that in the Greek Bible (the Septuagint) they appear in different positions within the book. Section VI appears as 24: 24–37 and 24: 50–68, while 31: 1–9 is 24: 69–77 and 31: 10–31 appears as 29: 28–49. These all are probably excerpts from other collections of Wisdom Literature. There is something artificial in their form and style, and this would suggest a late date. The poem on the Good Wife with its acrostic form suggests the time of Rabbinical methods in literature. We cannot escape the feeling that these late additions are somewhat alien to the general spirit of the book. The date of the book as we now have it must be later than the date of its latest section. In this case Section I seems to be latest in time and we saw reason to date that in the third century B.C. The book as we now have it cannot be earlier than that.

Authorship of Proverbs

So much for the literary plan of the book of Proverbs. A word, however, may be added as to the authorship attributed to Solomon. In 1 Kings 4: 30–34 we are told that Solomon excelled in wisdom and uttered 3000 proverbs, while in 1 Kings 10: 1–9 we learn how the Queen of Sheba was overwhelmed with his display of wisdom. Clearly Solomon was a monarch of wide interests and catholic sympathies and under his rule ample scope was afforded for cultural progress and intellectual advance. Furthermore, Solomon had marital ties with the Egyptian monarchy and there was much coming and going between these two countries. It was Israel's golden age and it was a period of literary activity in Israel: it was probably at this time that the earliest narratives of Israel's history were written down.

Solomon thus became, as it were, the patron saint of Wisdom just as Moses was regarded as the fount and source of Hebrew Law, and David as the father of music and song. There may be proverbs from Solomon in our book but we cannot identify them. For, truth to tell, proverbs have no father. No man can say, Go to, I will make a proverb. For proverbs are born and not made. The wind bloweth where it listeth and proverbs come unbidden and unexpected. For the true proverb is "the wit of one and the wisdom of many". Doctor Dryasdust might write for fifty years and never come up with the flash of insight that visited the country yokel who on a day long ago exclaimed, "Is Saul also among the prophets?" Or the peasant man who asked in his simplicity "What has the chaff to do with the wheat?" Such words cut like a blade of steel and reach to the centre of things. They reveal and expose to view the very heart of a matter: they uncover the vital situation in plain concrete terms. Brief, pithy, pungent, popular—these are the marks of the authentic proverb. In them we have the distilled wisdom of the ages, the spontaneous and immediate reaction of discerning spirits to the world around them.

That is why the book is difficult to read. There is no plan or systematic arrangement. Every one of them is ruggedly in-dividual, relentlessly separate from his fellow. There is no ordered march of a disciplined army here but rather the parade of guerrilla warriors, each on his own. And that is why, if we are wise, we will not take too big a dose at one sitting: we must diet ourselves here:

> If you have found honey, eat only enough for you,
> lest you be sated with it and vomit it.   (25 : 16.)

Enough is as good as a feast: honey is cloying and one can have too much of a good thing. And it may be in this way we shall come to see that these warriors after all are not an undisciplined host but rather a great army whose loyalty is to Wisdom, whose purpose is to establish laws of heaven for life on earth.

3. EXPOSITION OF THE BOOK

PERHAPS THE best way to grasp the content of this book is to begin with a study of the group to which its teachings were specially directed—the Fools. These meet us on almost every page and the word "fool" occurs more than a hundred times. One might conclude from this that there were more fools in Israel than elsewhere, but that is not so. It indicates rather the intensity and passion of the Sages who seek to increase wisdom.

We may now consider those pupils of the Sages: they are the unwise, the fools. They are the raw material on which the teacher had to work and they represent varying degrees of rawness. There are fools and fools, as we shall see from the various terms used.

The Teachable Fool

First there is the *Pethi*, translated "simple" (A.V. and R.S.V.). The word means "open" and thus signifies one who is open and accessible. The mind is not closed and barred against the entrance of wisdom. He is teachable. But everything depends on who gets him first—the Sage or Madame Folly. Influence may be brought to bear on such simpletons and the Sage is eager to bring the right influence that will shape and mould character:

> that prudence may be given to the simple,
> knowledge and discretion to the youth.   (1 : 4.)

But it is not natural for boys to love discipline and children may not want to go to school:

> How long, O simple ones, will you love being simple?
> (1 : 22.)

The mind cannot remain vacant: undesirable tenants may take occupancy here:

> I have seen among the simple, (*Pethi*)
> I have perceived among the youths,
>   a young man without sense, (*Chāsēr Lēb*)

Passing along the street near her corner,
taking the road to her (i.e. the harlot's) house. (7: 7, 8.)

Here we meet another word for fool (*Chāsēr Lēb*), which means "without sense" or more literally "lacking heart". The A.V. says "void of understanding". Perhaps we might use Shakespeare's term "Lackbrain" (*Henry IV*, pt. 1) and we must remember the Hebrew had no word for "brain". The Hebrew knew with the heart and the heart was the organ of intellection. "Lackbrain" always appears in parallelism with "simple" and is perhaps just another name for him. He lacks sense and is empty of understanding. But if he is open to temptation he is also open to instruction. There is hope for him:

When a scoffer (*Lētz*) is punished, the simple becomes wise;
(21: 11.)

The faults of *Pethi* and *Chāsēr Lēb* are the faults of youth. The Sages had their chance here and they did not neglect it. The simple could be educated and the Lackbrains could be given understanding—if the Sages caught them early.

The Hardened Fool

If they did not catch them early the last state of that man might well be worse than the first. For he might become a *Kěsīl* or an *Ěwīl*, two more advanced types of fool. The root meaning of these terms is similar, "to be thick or fat" and in a bad sense to be thickheaded. These are coarse and hardened fools with a strong degree of swinishness in their make-up. They "despise wisdom and instruction" (1: 7) and revel in their folly:

It is like sport to a fool to do wrong. (10: 23.)

Oblivious of moral and spiritual realities they trumpet abroad their pride and joy in evil doing:

> A prudent man conceal his knowledge,
> but fools proclaim their folly. (12: 23.)

They seek to create trouble and their loud mouths will always be a-brawling:

> It is an honour for a man to keep aloof from strife;
> but every fool will be quarrelling. (20: 3.)

We cannot but admire the patience and persistence of these teachers. Their job was not easy and it was performed with great travail of spirit. At times they must have almost despaired:

> A rebuke goes deeper into a man of understanding
> than a hundred blows into a fool. (17: 10.)

Neither through the pores of their skin nor through the avenues of their hardened hearts could one drive in wisdom: they were mentally immune to instruction:

> Crush a fool in a mortar with a pestle . . .
> yet his folly will not depart from him. (27: 22.)

The Sages must often have felt like using force against these loud-mouthed rowdies but what chance did those gentle humanists have against such thickheads? And they were wise enough to recognize that

> He who is slow to anger is better than the mighty,
> and he who rules his spirit than he who takes a city.
> (16: 32.)

The Arrogant Fool

A fifth type is found in the _Lētz_, generally translated "scoffer" or "scorner". This is the arrogant type who turns his back on the Sage and spurns his teaching. He knows all the answers: none can teach him. He is something of a highbrow who would scorn to be associated with the swinish *Kesil* or *Ewil*. He is a cut above that kind of thing: he knows too much. Nevertheless he lacks real wisdom:

> "Scoffer" is the name of the proud, haughty man
> who acts with arrogant pride.   (21 : 24.)

There is no pride like pride of intellect and here the Sages found their most formidable foes. For they were subtle in argument and unscrupulous in debate, and frequently the Sage was non-plussed and confounded by them. They were past masters in the art of heckling and they rejoiced with malicious joy to disrupt a meeting:

> Scoffers set a city aflame,
> but wise men turn away wrath.   (29 : 8.)

What purpose did such scoffers serve in a moral universe? But the Sages still believed in such a universe:

> Drive out a scoffer, and strife will go out,
> and quarrelling and abuse will cease.   (22 : 10.)

They were hated by their fellow men and God Himself finds no pleasure in them:

> Toward the scorners he is scornful,
> but to the humble he shows favour.   (3 : 34.)

Last scene of all that ends this strange story—the *Nābāl*. He is mentioned only four times but finds himself more fully documented in 1 Samuel 25 : 25. Fool by name and fool by nature, here we have the churl dead to all decency and order. Devoid of intellectual interest and religious faith, he says "There is no

67

God" (Psalm 14 : 1). The *Lētz* sparkles in his devilish cleverness but the Nābāl repels us with his brutish sottishness.

Clearly the Sages worked with raw material and at times they felt altogether frustrated and at their wits'end :

> A whip for the horse, a bridle for the ass,
>   and a rod for the back of fools.   (26 : 3.)

To expel the vestigial remains of "the ape and tiger"—and the donkey that still remained in man—they strongly advocated the use of the rod :

> Do not withhold discipline from a child;
>   If you beat him with a rod, he will not die.
> If you beat him with the rod
>   you will save his life from Sheol.   (23 : 13, 14.)

Wise words are these from the Sages and we are thankful for them.

Education According to The Sages

This, then, was the sphere in which the Sages carried on their task of education. We generally assume that this word is derived from the Latin "edūco", *I lead forth,* and we think education is the process by which we lead forth innate ideas in the child mind. We have systems of education grounded on this idea : the value of such systems may be questioned. The word "education" is not derived from *edūco, I lead forth,* but from *edŭco, I plant or produce.* We should know enough about the Romans to recognize that originally they were peasant farmers and that they planted seed and produced crops. We speak of a school as a *seminary* and that word comes from the Latin word *semen,* meaning seed. It is a place where seed is sown in young minds in the hope that later on it will produce a crop, and yield a harvest in the realm of character. Is not this what Thackeray had in mind when he wrote:

Sow a thought, reap an act; sow an act, reap a habit;
sow a habit, reap character; sow character, reap destiny.

Is not this what the Sage had in mind when he wrote:

Train up a child in the way he should go,
    and when he is old he will not depart from it.   (22 : 6.)

The word here used for "train" is the root of the Hebrew word
for education (*Chinnucah*). The present writer has taught most
of his life in a theological seminary and has been reasonably
certain about the quality of the seed he was sowing. It was
imported from Scotland and deemed to be of prime quality.
But while he has not doubted the quality of the seed he has at
times had misgivings about the soils in which it was planted.
Some were good and some were not so good. The harvest
varied. That must always be so. But the Sages laboured dili-
gently at the sowing, and like the present writer they enjoyed
this education. Paul may plant and Apollos water but it is God
who gives the increase. And like Paul and Apollos the Sages
had the ecumenical vision: their teaching was for Everyman:

To you, O men, I call,
    and my cry is to the sons of men.   (8 : 4.)

Wisdom addresses all men. Wisdom is the true cosmopolitan:
there is no colour bar here. The Hebrew Humanists believed
with Pope that "the proper study of mankind is man". This
ecumenical purpose and this view of the distant horizon gave a
joyous uplift to those teachers and their teaching. There breathes
about it an air of optimism and though at times the teaching may
seem rather prudential and with all the marks of worldly wisdom
upon it we may not forget that it is all undergirded and sustained by a strong religious foundation.

"The fear of the Lord is the beginning of wisdom." This is
not paraded like a banner headline but it is assumed on every

page and forms a deep undertone throughout the book. Here we have no Doctors Dryasdust reciting outworn dogmas but morning voices that speak in words that ring like iron and shine like gold. The Sages rejoiced in life and its opportunities:

> The light of the eyes rejoices the heart,
> and good news refreshes the bones. (15: 30.)

It was God's world in which men lived and moved and had their being, and it was bliss to be alive in God's world.

Wisdom—President of the World

For it was a world of good order and purpose. It was a world imbued with Wisdom, and the path of life for men lay in finding this Wisdom. The world was not a chaos but a cosmos and Wisdom presided at its founding. Wisdom was of the very essence of God, and surely Paul had this in mind when he spoke of Christ as the Wisdom of God (1 Corinthians 1: 24). In the bold personalization of Wisdom in 8: 22f. the writer is restating the fundamental truths set forth in the first two chapters of Genesis. There we learn that behind the universe is a Person and that the world is not the result of chance but the determination of a Creator, and that the Creator has a purpose:

> The Lord by wisdom founded the earth;
> by understanding he established the heavens.
>   (3: 19.)

Everything in the creative process is marked by deliberation and design:

> The hearing ear and the seeing eye,
> the Lord has made them both. (20: 12.)

And the creative process finds its culmination in man, made in the image of God. Furthermore, God is profoundly interested in man, in his education, and welfare:

> Hear instruction and be wise,
> and do not neglect it. (8 : 33.)

God has given man work to do, laws to obey, a conscience to respect, and a companion helper to aid him in the achievement of his high destiny. Man is not only God's creature: he is God's friend.

> The spirit of man is the lamp of the Lord,
> searching all his innermost parts. (20 : 27.)

That is how the Sages saw the world and they rejoiced with radiant Wisdom who dwelt, and came forth from, God:

> I was daily his delight,
> rejoicing before him always,
> rejoicing in his inhabited world
> and delighting in the sons of men.
>
> (8 : 30, 31.)

The Sages shared this joy and found their delight in the sons of men:

> The glory of young men is their strength,
> but the beauty of old men is their grey hair.
>
> (20 : 29.)

Everything is beautiful in its season, for God has ordained it so. And, if man by folly has lost Eden, work need not be a curse:

> Love not sleep, lest you come to poverty;
> open your eyes, and you will have plenty of bread.
>
> (20 : 13.)

71

"A man's task is his life preserver" and God blesses man's toil:

> In all toil there is profit,
> but mere talk tends only to want.   (14: 23.)

There is perhaps no more realistic word in the whole book than just this:

> A worker's appetite works for him;
> his mouth urges him on.   (16: 26.)

That gets down to brass tacks, as we say, and we do not need Paul to tell us that if a man will not work he may not eat (2 Thessalonians 3: 10). The prophets might have their heads in the air but the Sages had their feet on the ground and dealt with real life in realistic fashion. There is a certain ruthlessness in their attitude to the slacker:

> Go to the ant, O sluggard;
> consider her ways, and be wise.   (6: 6.)

It may be that we have taken that counsel too much to heart and our modern industrial system is the result. That may well give us pause. For man is more than an ant. And to make a life is more than to make a living. We live to-day in a money-culture where the heart of man is set on material things. Man does not live by bread alone but assuredly he cannot live without it. Materialism as a system fails to satisfy because it believes material things are the only things. And here the Sage will again speak to our condition:

> Two things I ask of thee;
> deny them not to me before I die:
> Remove far from me falsehood and lying;
> give me neither poverty nor riches;
> feed me with the food that is needful for me,

Lest I be full, and deny thee,
 and say, "Who is the Lord?"
Or lest I be poor, and steal,
 and profane the name of my God. (30: 7–9.)

The Golden Mean of Moderation

The Sages sought the Golden Mean and here they come close to
the Greek ideal of moderation in all things, "nothing too much".
But they lived in a world where man's inhumanity to man made
such an ideal impossible. Wealth tended to accumulate and men
decayed and though we miss here the prophetic passion we are
still conscious of long-prevailing social ills:

There are those whose teeth are swords,
 whose teeth are knives,
to devour the poor from off the earth,
 the needy from among men. (30: 14.)

"Field was laid to field" by unjust seizure and main force:

Do not remove an ancient landmark
 or enter the fields of the fatherless.
       (23: 10, cf. 22: 28.)

The lot of the poor was hard and no remedy seemed near:

The poor use entreaties,
 but the rich answer roughly. (18: 23.)

Even where sympathy might be expected it was not forth-
coming:

All a poor man's brothers hate him;
 how much more do his friends go far from him!
        (19: 7.)

Wealth brings many new friends,
    but a poor man is deserted by his friend.   (19: 4.)

But The Sage still believed in a world ruled by a righteous God:

He who mocks the poor insults his Maker;
    he who is glad at calamity will not go unpunished.
                                               (17: 5.)

We speak of Capital and Labour, Riches and Poverty, and behind
these abstract terms the real problem tends to be hidden. The
Sages speak of the Poor Man and the Rich Man and we see the
problem before our eyes. It may be that to-day we emphasize
too much the dangers of Poverty and forget the greater prominence which both the Sages and our Lord gave to the danger
of Riches. "A penny held close enough to the eye will obscure
the whole universe." So said Juliana of Norwich. Riches may
come between a man and God:

A rich man's wealth is his strong city.   (10: 15.)

As Jeremy Taylor puts it, a man may go forward in the accounts
of time, but what about his standing in the accounts of eternity?
Dives may have thought Lazarus was just a part of the landscape
of his luxurious domains (Luke 16: 20), but the Sages denounced
such inhumane conduct. Like our Lord they knew that by
deeds of charity the currency of earth could be transformed
into treasure in heaven:

He who is kind to the poor lends to the Lord,
    and he will repay him for his deed.   (19: 17.)

And we may not forget our common humanity:

The rich and the poor meet together:
    the Lord is the maker of them all.   (22: 2.)

What a text for the Sages to develop! But the development had to await the coming of the master Sage who gave an ampler interpretation to the Fatherhood of God and the Brotherhood of Man.

Counsels of the Sages

We may now pass from this general background and consider some of the counsels given by the Sages. We will refer to them as (a) individual types, (b) domestic relations, (c) social requirements, and (d) political allegiance. It may be difficult to separate these clearly for man lives in social and political relations. But such a division may serve to show various aspects of the teaching. Many sayings will slip through the meshes of our net but we should make a good catch that may yield food for thought. (a) *Individual types*. Slander seems to flourish everywhere and, as in Egypt and Babylon, we find it rife in the Holy City.

> A perverse man spreads strife,
>> and a whisperer separates close friends.   (16 : 28.)

And surely it is a wise word that tells us that

> He who keeps his mouth and his tongue
>> keeps himself out of trouble.   (21 : 23.)

The Scots might match that last saying with "Shut mouths catch no flies", and that takes care of moral and sanitary laws. Best of all and hitting the nail on the head is this word:

> For lack of wood the fire goes out;
>> and where there is no whisperer, quarrelling ceases.
>>> (26 : 20.)

There is always danger that we may speak in anger and repent at leisure. So bear it in mind:

A soft answer turns away wrath,
  but a harsh word stirs up anger.   (15: 1.)

The greatest victory we can ever win is the victory over self: it is the hardest of all to gain:

Do you see a man who is wise in his own eyes?
  there is more hope for a fool (*Kesil*) than for him.
        (26: 12.)

Nor may we omit this:

For pressing milk produces curds,
  pressing the nose produces blood,
  and pressing anger produces strife.   (30: 33.)

These old Sages had more in their head than hair. Nothing escaped their observation and often their words ring like silver bells:

Like clouds and wind without rain
  is a man who boasts of a gift he does not give.
        (25: 14.)

One feels inclined to comment on that with a Hindu Proverb:

Words are the daughters of earth,
  but deeds are the sons of heaven.

A more subtle form of this failing is revealed in:

One man pretends to be rich, yet has nothing:
  another pretends to be poor, yet has great wealth.
        (13: 7.)

These are all shams, hollow men: The Sage seeks reality.

A more mundane concern might seem the question of prudence and tact. But many Christian lives have been robbed of their charm by lack of these qualities:

> Answer not a fool according to his folly,
> lest you be like him yourself. (26: 4.)

Perhaps the Sage had learned that from his own experience. Even Homer may nod. And yet again

> He who sings songs to a heavy heart
> is like one who takes off a garment on a cold day,
> and like vinegar on a wound. (25: 20.)

Sometimes this may become positively disgusting:

> Like a gold ring in a swine's snout
> is a beautiful woman without discretion.
>   (11: 22.)

Evidently there were quite a few of these in old Jerusalem. A man had to watch his step:

> A prudent man sees danger and hides himself;
> but the simple go on, and suffer for it. (22: 3.)

Discretion may be the better part of valour. Nor is it wise to believe all one hears:

> The simple believes everything,
> but the prudent looks where he is going. (14: 15.)

It is certainly not easy to carry on any ministry or form of Christian service without a sense of humour. The Sages saw much to provoke laughter. We are all bargain-hunters and we can visualize this scene:

> "It is naught, it is naught" saith the buyer;
> but when he is gone his way, then he boasteth.
>
> (20 : 14 A.V.)

A visit to a second-hand bookshop may often prove rewarding: if one follows the procedure indicated he may come forth "rejoicing as one who has found great spoil". But one must be careful not to kill the goose that lays the golden eggs! And what a laugh the Sage had when he looked on the lazy hunter who failed to complete his job and harvest the gains:

> The slothful man roasteth not that
> which he took in hunting.   (12 : 27 A.V.)

To bring down the buck and fail to take it home—how lazy can some folk be! Perhaps humour turns to satire in:

> As a door turns on its hinges,
> so does a sluggard on his bed,
> The sluggard buries his hand in the dish;
> it wears him out to bring it back to his mouth.
>
> (26 : 14, 15.)

But the Sage had little place for the practical joker: they can be so annoying and pestiferous:

> Like a madman who throws firebrands, arrows, and death,
> is the man who deceives his neighbour and says,
> "I am only joking!"   (26 : 18, 19.)

(b) *Domestic relations.* Every wise teacher knows that the foundation of national glory is in the homes of the people. And no people in all the world laid such stress on the proper upbringing of children. This is a main theme of the Sages, and to-day when all lament the decay of the home and the growth of juvenile delinquency it is well that we should give heed to their words:

> A wise son makes a glad father,
>> but a foolish son is a sorrow to his mother.   (10: 1.)

> The father of the righteous will greatly rejoice;
>> he who begets a wise son will be glad in him.
> Let your father and mother be glad,
>> let her who bore you rejoice.   (23: 24, 25)

That is the ideal and it was often realized in Jewish homes: it was so in the home at Nazareth. It is worthy of note that both father and mother are mentioned together—daughters are not mentioned at all—and all through the book of Proverbs a worthy place is accorded the wife and mother. Sometimes, however, their mutual joy might be marred by unworthy conduct on the part of their offspring:

> A stupid son is a grief to his father;
>> and the father of a fool has no joy.   (17: 21.)

> A foolish son is a grief to his father
>> and bitterness to her who bore him.   (17: 25.)

Sometimes waywardness might assume serious proportions:

> He who does violence to his father and chases away his mother
> is a son who causes shame and brings reproach.   (19: 26.)

We would hope this was the exception rather than the rule, but in the time of our Lord children seem to have learned the ignoble art of disinheriting parents:

> For Moses said, "Honour your father and your mother";
> and, "He who speaks evil of father or mother, let him
> surely die"; but you say, "If a man tells his father
> or his mother, What you would have gained from me
> is Corban" (that is, given to God)—then you no longer
> permit him to do anything for his father or mother.
>> (Mark 7: 10–12.)

Happier far the man of whom it could be said:

> A righteous man who walks in his integrity—
> blessed are his sons after him! (20: 7.)

There is an entail of goodness as there is an entail of evil. And we thank God that it is so.

The Jewish home could be disrupted by internal strife:

> A foolish son is ruin to his father,
> and a wife's quarrelling is a continual dripping of rain.
> (19: 13.)

And in these days it was not possible for folk to turn to the psychiatrist! Where there is smoke there is sure to be fire and all too often the nagging wife could drive her spouse to the point of exasperation:

> A continual dripping on a rainy day
> and a contentious woman are alike;
> to restrain her is to restrain the wind
> or to grasp oil in his right hand. (27: 15, 16.)

If there be any proverbs from Solomon in this book surely this must be one:

> It is better to dwell in a corner of the housetop,
> than with a brawling woman in a wide house.
> (21: 9 A.V.)

And who should know better than Solomon? But, on balance, the Sage knew that woman was "the better half" and that "a prudent wife is from the Lord" (19: 14). "Her price is above rubies" (31: 10) and her influence reaches far:

> Charm is deceitful, and beauty is vain,
> but a woman who fears the Lord is to be praised.
> (31: 30.)

So let the last word here be this:

> He who finds a wife finds a good thing,
>> and obtains favour from the Lord. (18 : 22.)

(c) *Social Requirements.* Here, too, we may learn something of Hebrew Social Life. The Sage knows that one can have too much of a good thing and so here he sets due bounds:

> Withdraw thy foot from thy neighbour's house;
>> lest he be weary of thee, and so hate thee.
>>> (25 : 17 A.V.)

Furthermore, there should be a principle of selectivity here. We must not cast our pearls—even if they be only simulated or artificial pearls—before swine lest they turn and rend us:

> Make no friendship with a man given to anger,
>> nor go with a wrathful man,
> lest you learn his ways
>> and entangle yourself in a snare. (22 : 24, 25.)

Evil communications corrupt good manners and some friendships are hollow and unreal:

> There are friends who pretend to be friends,
>> but there is a friend who sticks closer than a brother.
>>> (18 : 24.)

Again we must be wise as serpents and "discern the spirits":

> Faithful are the wounds of a friend;
>> profuse are the kisses of an enemy. (27 : 6.)

and above all keep your friendships in repair:

> Your friend, and your father's friend, do not forsake.
>> (27 : 10.)

(d) *Political allegiance*. In the political sphere man should act warily and be duly subject to the powers that be ordained of God:

> The king's heart is a stream of water in the hand of the Lord;
> he turns it wherever he will.   (21 : 1.)

Render to Caesar the things that are Caesar's and fail not to give God His due. The Sage may have had the ideal in view when he wrote:

> It is an abomination to kings to do evil,
> for the throne is established by righteousness.
> (16 : 12.)

But the Sage is realistic enough to know that

> Like a roaring lion or a charging bear
> is a wicked ruler over a poor people.   (28 : 15.)

The folk who lived and died under Antiochus the Madman could say "Amen" to that, and they would long eagerly for the coming of One of whom they could say truthfully

> Inspired decisions are on the lips of a king;
> his mouth does not sin in judgment.   (16 : 10.)

Like the seers and singers of old Israel, the Sage holds up a mirror for magistrates:

> If a king judges the poor with equity
> his throne will be established for ever.   (29 : 14.)

Even amid the brute facts of life the Sage holds to his ideal:

Take away the wicked from the presence of the king,
    and his throne will be established in righteousness.

(25: 5.)

Let not man needlessly provoke the monarch, for

> A king's wrath is like the growling of a lion,
>   but his favour is like dew upon the grass.   (19: 12.)

And life would be highly unpleasant without the dew on the grass.

Nothing lies outside the range of the Sages' teaching: good manners are a sign of real godliness:

> When you sit down to eat with a ruler,
>   observe carefully what is before you;
> And put a knife to your throat
>   if you are a man given to appetite.   (23 : 1, 2.)

A cat may look at the king and that is probably as far as most of us will ever attain. But we should always comport ourselves as if we were in the king's presence and on our own lower levels we shall at least act like gentlefolk. And in case you may come to the highest honour and be called to the royal presence do not forget this word:

> Do not put yourself forward in the king's presence
>   or stand in the place of the great;
> for it is better to be told, "Come up here",
>   than to be put lower in the presence of the prince.

(25: 6, 7.)

That needs no commentary—but remember the text! Perhaps there is another side to this—the Sage knew both sides, or was it another Sage—and it may be that the children of this world know something more than the children of light:

> A man's gift makes room for him
>> and brings him before great men.   (18 : 16.)

And maybe it is best to be on the safe side :

> A gift in secret averts anger;
>> and a bribe in the bosom, strong wrath.   (21 : 14.)

But let a man have a care, for he must keep the peace with his own conscience. A bribe may be "a magic stone in the eyes of him who gives it "(17 : 18) but more often it proves a "stone of stumbling". A people's highest welfare lies in its spiritual soundness :

> Righteousness exalts a nation,
>> but sin is a reproach to any people.   (14 : 34.)

The wide sympathies of the Sages reached also to the animal creation :

> A righteous man has regard for the life of his beast,
>> but the mercy of the wicked is cruel.   (12 : 10.)

As the Rhode Island farmer said, "When I got religion even the cat knew about it." And that is as it should be.

> He prayeth best who loveth best
>> All things both great and small;
> For the dear God who loveth us,
>> He made and loveth all.   (Coleridge.)

Religion to the Sage is a total commitment; there can be no un-redeemed areas in the life of him who fears the Lord.

"Hast thou found honey." Lest we become surfeited with overmuch food of this kind we will call a halt by looking briefly at some evils to avoid and some virtues to cherish.

He who belittles his neighbour lacks sense,
  but a man of understanding remains silent.

(11 : 12.)

If we can say nothing good let us keep our mouth shut. And let us behave decently as Christians:

If a man returns evil for good,
  evil will not depart from his house.   (17 : 13.)

Assuredly the human heart is desperately wicked and at times we can be awfully mean:

Like the glaze covering an earthen vessel
  are smooth lips with an evil heart.   (26 : 23.)

And again have a care, for

He that winketh with the eye causeth sorrow;
  but a prating fool shall fall.   (10 : 10 A.V.)

But look at the other side of the ledger:

The tongue of the righteous is choice silver;
  the mind of the wicked is of little worth.   (10 : 20.)

The Language of The Sages

The Sages may seem to speak a different language from the priests and prophets. There are no words here like Circumcision, Sabbath, or even the Temple. The word repentance, so frequent in the prophets, is not found here. But let it be said here that these Sages are no less religious than those other more conspicuous servants of God. Nor are they less concerned with the spiritual life. They, too, set forth in their own way the real marrow of divinity, the essence of religion. In a quiet unobtrusive style they set forth God's relation to man and man's duty towards God:

> To do righteousness and justice
> > is more acceptable to the Lord than sacrifice.   (21 : 3.)

There they stand in the prophetic succession and see things straight:

> A liberal man will be enriched,
> > and one who waters will himself be watered.
> > > (11 : 25.)

Religion finds expression in service, and by their fruits men are known. We may sum it up in this word:

> Let not loyalty and faithfulness forsake you;
> > bind them about your neck . . .
> So you will find favour and good repute
> > in the sight of God and man.   (3 : 3, 4.)

To grow in favour with God and man—what more can we ask?

Enough has been adduced in the foregoing to indicate the real character and significance of the book of Proverbs. We may feel that here we are dealing with prudential morality and that much of this could be matched by the Wisdom literature of other peoples. That is true. Israel was not "a peculiar people" in that sense. Wisdom literature was a universal phenomenon.

The Place of Proverbs

As to the charge that all this seems on a fairly low level one or two things should be said. Firstly we must admit there is much that seems mere worldly wisdom, and that there is no sense of absolute moral law. Also, that the emphasis is on the passive virtues—courage is not mentioned—and that the prevailing thought is utilitarian and of worldly happiness dealing with material welfare. Moreover it is objected that there is no strong sense of social responsibility, and that the main emphasis is egotistic.

We may take the last point first. Here we are concerned with a paradox in the Semitic character. That character is composed of various striking paradoxes and one of the most striking is this. The Semite shows a distinct subjectiveness to the phenomena of Nature and History and at the same time a strange objectiveness in describing them. This may be observed all through the Old Testament and it is easy to understand. For the desert is a place of danger. The attitude of the desert-dweller must always be that of the sentinel. There a man must always stand at the alert and he must interrogate every sight or sound in relation to himself and his safety. Otherwise he will not be long in the land of the living. Wild beasts and wilder men lie in wait to rob him of life. Thus the desert-dweller has developed an uncanny self-regarding instinct: his first question must always be, What does this mean for me? That instinct has been ground into the character through millennia of time and it is not difficult to see how a sense of world service was little likely to take root in such soil. The Sages were realists and their approach was wise.

Further, objection is made to the utilitarian conception employed in this approach. Thus Wisdom says:

> I walk in the way of righteousness,
>   in the paths of justice,
> endowing with wealth those who love me,
>   and filling their treasuries. (8: 20, 21.)

Piety brings prosperity. Religion is profitable. This idea we have already seen in our study of Job. But there is more truth in this old philosophy than we may be prepared to admit. It is true over a wide area that

> He who gives heed to the word will prosper,
>   and happy is he who trusts in the Lord. (16: 20.)

The Hebrew had practically no view of a life hereafter—such a belief was late in arriving—and if the idea of a righteous God was to be maintained then the divine justice must be revealed in the present life. And that was so in most instances. Christianity itself is frequently assailed on this same ground, that we teach people to be good for the sake of a reward. And why not? It is difficult to see how we can dispense with the thought of reward; Christ offered large rewards to His followers (Mark 10: 29) and Paul rightly assures us that "godliness is profitable unto all things" (1 Timothy 4: 8 A.V.). Man has a right to expect profit from religion and it will be time enough to consider this objection seriously when we find those who make the objection living the Christian life without thought of the Christian reward.

Influence on Christian Teaching

It may be observed that although the book is rarely quoted directly by our Lord there can be no question it exercised a large influence both upon the form and content of His teaching. Like the Sages He taught in the streets, in the fields, and by the seaside. No Gospel writer is more concerned than Matthew to show the close connection of the Old and New Testaments: to Matthew Jesus is the fulfilment and completion of the Old Testament. The parable of the two houses (Matthew 7: 24f.) reminds us of the Sages' teaching:

> The wicked are overthrown and are no more,
> but the house of the righteous will stand. (12: 7.)

The parable in Luke 14: 7–11 is an expansion of Proverbs 25: 6, 7 where men are warned against taking the best seats at a banquet. Quite striking is the word of Peter—and who should know better —when he writes:

> Love covers a multitude of sins. (1 Peter 4: 8.)

This is surely an echo of the Sages:

> Hatred stirs up strife,
> but love covers all offences.   (10: 12.)

James, also, who is likest to a sage in the New Testament, could not pass by that beautiful word:

> Whoever brings back a sinner from the error
> of his way will save his soul from death
> and will cover a multitude of sins.   (James 5: 20.)

"Give us our daily bread" is but another form of the prayer in Proverbs 30: 8, "feed me with the bread of my portion". From these and many other parallels we may justly conclude that our Lord refreshed His spirit at this ancient fount of Wisdom. We may not forget that the Old Testament was the Bible of our Lord and what was precious to the Redeemer can never be less than precious to the redeemed.

A Manual of Ethics

This writer recalls with pride and affection a home where this book was the manual of ethics and its precepts were graven deep on his heart. As he looks back now he is very sure that the value of this book, the element that makes it Holy Scripture, is just the genuine piety and real religion of the Sages. Deep calleth unto deep. And water does not rise above its own level. Religion here in humble garb enters in at lowly doors. The enthusiasm of the Sages—and none may mistake it—in the pursuit of Wisdom, which is of God and with God, which is both the root and the fruit of all good living, plainly attests the sincere piety and devoted service of those teachers.

> The fear of the Lord is the beginning of wisdom,
> and the knowledge of the Holy One is insight.
> (9: 10.,

All their teaching rests on belief in the great and holy God, source of all Wisdom, who alone can direct men to a meaningful and satisfying way of life. No aspect of life, manners or morals, lies outside their purview. Every thought and every activity is to be brought under the sole sovereign sway of that Wisdom "by whom kings reign, and princes decree justice" (8 : 16). The teaching may seem commonplace to us—it may even suggest salvation by works or merit—but that is precisely because we so seldom think of religion as total commitment in which no unredeemed areas remain. When we see religion thus as the Sages saw it and taught it we will not again speak of anything "as common or unclean":

> Trust in the Lord with all your heart,
>   and do not rely on your own insight.   (3 : 5.)

Let there be no mistake here, and let the last word be as the first:

> Wisdom is the principal thing;
>   therefore get wisdom,
>   and with all thy getting get understanding.
>   (4 : 7, A.V.)

It may cost all we have. But "What shall it profit a man if he gain the whole world and lose his own soul?" That is the voice of the Master Sage.

4. POWER OF THE BOOK

SOMETHING HAS already been said as to the influence of the Sages on their own time and that influence is attested by the presence of the book in the Old Testament. We have shown also its continuing influence both in the form and content of our Lord's teaching and in the writings of the New Testament. This also is part of our Christian heritage and we are heirs of all the promises. Here, however, we raise the question of its power and influence in our own time. What do these counsels and admonitions signify for us to-day?

These Timeless Counsels

Times have changed greatly since these counsels were first given. To-day as we look back over the present century and think of our fathers who lived before the coming of the auto-mobile and the aeroplane and all the modern gadgets that fill our homes we wonder how they lived. It is like looking across the great divide. Between them and us a great gulf is fixed. We live in a different world, in the nuclear age when men range the skies and seek to visit the moon. We "have sought out many inventions" and made so many discoveries that the mind of man is overwhelmed with new and disturbing prospects. We are proud of our attainments and have reached a point where modern nations seem to be engaged in the worship of their own handiwork and, like the proud Assyrians, we "sacrifice to our net and burn incense to our seine" (Habakkuk 1 : 16). We live under the tyranny of tools and "things ride the man". Great nations have repudiated the very idea of God and have developed civilizations in which moral and spiritual values seem to be totally eclipsed. The ancient landmarks have been removed and we have lost our bearings. Cold wars threaten to erupt into shoot-ing wars and the awakening east looks as if it might finally engulf a morally decadent west. The air is full of rumours and while men say, "Lo, here" or "Lo, there" no one knows what a day may bring forth. We seem to live "on the brink" and men's hearts tremble as trees before the autumn gales.

All this seems to indicate that our moral progress has not kept up with our technological advance. Men's scientific discoveries have not been matched by equal attainments in the realm of moral and spiritual values. There has been a strange decay in character and a lamentable decline in public and private morality. In England the publication of *English Life and Leisure* by Seebohm Rowntree and G. R. Lavers alarmed discerning people by its amazing revelations of the extent of this decline. In America the Catholic Congress recently made bold to say that in America life seemed to be like that of Rome before its fall when the popular demand was for nothing but "bread and circuses".

There is an old tale from Denmark that tells of a spider that had built its home in the high rafters of a building where it was bleak and cold and food was not too plentiful. One day the spider spun its thread and descended to a lower level where there was food aplenty and flies to catch. It waxed fat and prospered. One day it looked up and saw the thin-spun thread that bound it to its home. "What's the use of that", it said, and slit the thread. It went crashing to the ground to be trodden under foot of men. We offer that in the spirit of the Sages who loved parables. And a word to the wise may not go unheeded.

Inherited Faith and New Dynamic

We do not mean to say that Materialism is all wrong. In doing so we would condemn the Sages. Materialism is not wrong in thinking of material things but it is fundamentally wrong in thinking that material things are the only things. The Sages did not make that mistake. Like ourselves they lived in a time of transition and they found the period of transition fraught with danger to the only way of life they believed worth living. New ideas were in the air and were coming from all quarters. More particularly there was to the west of them another great civilization that refused to stay within its borders. We refer to Greece. To that people we owe a very great debt. From the Greeks we have received those impulses that created and moulded western civilization. Greece is the home of art, science, and philosophy and from it we have received the idea of democracy. We would not in any way derogate from the greatness of that heritage: countless volumes make clear to us our debt to Greece.

They were a people with a passion for freedom, a love of adventure, and a mind to explore everything in earth or heaven. When, in the course of history, this civilization came face to face with that of the Hebrew something significant emerged. The conflict of Hebraism and Hellenism is not unlike that in which we are involved to-day.

For the Sages were provoked to their ministry by a conflict, the conflict between an inherited faith and a new dynamic ideology. When Alexander the Great set forth in 334 B.C. to conquer Asia a new era dawned in the ancient world. For Alexander's purpose was not merely to conquer territory but to spread Greek culture and to import something wholly new and different into Asia. This was done deliberately by a gradual infiltration, by building Greek cities and by the introduction of the Greek way of life. A dynamic form was set side by side with the static form of Semitic life. For Semitic life was unchanging and is still so to-day. The Semite is characterized by a marvellous patience and will endure almost any conditions of political and economic life. The deeply ingrained habit of acquiescence in the *status quo* prevented Semitic political development while the lively vital character of the Greek was for ever seeking after something new. When Paul visited Athens it was this searching inquisitive nature that intrigued him:

> All the Athenians and the foreigners who
> lived there spent their time in nothing
> except telling or hearing something new.
>
> (Acts 17: 21.)

The last thing the Hebrews desired was innovation: their unfailing response to anything new was "It hath not been so wrought in Israel heretofore".

The Clash of Cultures

This was the background of the Sages' teaching. They were called upon to build a bridge between the old and the new and to mould the emerging character of Judaism. The methods of Alexander were peaceful but his successors sought to force things by the power of the sword. Hence came the Maccabean wars. Doubtless there was much that was attractive in the Greek way of life, and its display did not fail to influence Hebrew youth. The public gymnasia, the athletic contests, the general free and easy life, and the wearing of the broad-brimmed hat and the fluttering cloak broached about the shoulders—all these laid a spell on Hebrew youth. This life, too, was not lacking in gaiety. Moreover the Greeks were a conquering people and a man has to live. One may not forget "on which side his bread is buttered". Why be conservative and stubborn when good jobs were available? Had not old Ptah-hotep counselled that way? But evil communications corrupt good manners. And all was not sound in Greek culture. It was a civilization based on slavery and contempt for work. Moreover it lacked moral idealism. And as so often happens in such cases it was mainly the less worthy features that were transferred and life in Syrian towns became, for the most part, a gratification of the grosser senses. Madame Folly appeared in many new guises and false philosophies threatened to seduce the Jews from their main loyalty, "the fear of the Lord". Conflicts such as these are ultimately spiritual: our warfare is against principalities and powers and against spiritual wickedness in high places. And it was precisely because the Sages had a deeper and profounder conception of man and his world that the Hebrew proved mightier than the Greek (Zechariah 9 : 13). *For the Greek did not have "the fear of the Lord".*

History is Judgment

The solemn truth is clear for all to see. The history of the world is the judgment of the world. No nation and no civilization can endure save as it has a real spiritual foundation. To make a nation or civilization three things are needed; (1) a people, (2) a land, (3) a spiritual principle. Those great empires of the east that marched and countermarched up and down the Way of the Sea, with nothing to satisfy but their own hot, greedy, snatching appetites, are all gone. To-day the archaeologist is digging in the dust to find the place where once they were. They were great material masses held together by physical power and when a greater mass came against them they were broken and dissolved. The glory that was Greece and the grandeur that was Rome shared the same fate as Babylon, Assyria, and Persia. And more recent empires have followed in their train. And as God lives and reigns so will it ever be. But Israel still abides. It has stood by the grave of all its oppressors and been the mordant critic of every civilization. Why? Again let us say it: these empires were founded on brute force and in them there was no truth, no righteousness, no mercy. Israel, on the other hand, has been a people oppressed and buffeted, and at times without a land. But such was the strength of the spiritual principle, or what Abraham Lincoln called "the product of a proposition", that it has survived the slings and arrows of outrageous fortune. *It had a spiritual core at the centre of its life.*

That spiritual principle gave meaning to history and significance to the life of the individual. That principle may be found in the promise to Abraham, "I will bless thee, that in thee all nations may be blessed". And that is the message of Israel. It has ecumenical significance. For it is a message of truth and righteousness and mercy. All these words are central in the teaching of the Sages, and they are central in the message of the Gospel. These are "the things by which men live and wholly therein is the life of the spirit". "Religion is the opiate of the masses," said Karl Marx, and great republics have been built on that basis. But they shall not stand. Man does not live by bread alone, and the human heart, in which God hath set eternity, can never be satisfied with the things of time and sense.

Madame Folly comes again to us to-day in the form of cunningly devised philosophies and alien ideologies. Folly is sustained with the doctrines of men. But Wisdom is still crying in the streets and her address is to "the sons of men". And a greater than Solomon has come, and to us he is the Wisdom and the power of God. "He that hath ears, let him hear". Righteousness alone exalteth a nation: God has built that principle into the fabric of the universe and Wisdom is justified of her children. "Other foundation can no man lay than that which is laid".